DAY TRADING

FOR BEGINNERS

How to make money in 14 days, the best
strategies step by step to maximize your profit
and build your financial income for living

LUCAS SHELTON

Table of Contents

Introduction... 4

Chapter One 9

Chapter Two...21

Chapter Three..42

Chapter Four 52

Chapter Five 69

Chapter Six 87

Chapter Seven..95

Conclusion..108

Introduction

The stock markets used to have such big swings that it was easy to buy and sell online stocks every day and make a lot of money. During that brief period of time, day traders made a lot of money trading tech company stocks. The tech index, NASDAQ, was soaring at the time, increasing thousands of points in a few of months. Because there was a tremendous wave in the IT ocean, and traders were riding it, day trading was a thriving business. When the dot-com bubble burst and markets reverted to their normal trading patterns, day trading became less profitable. However, for many others, it remained a fulfilling career.

During the Dot-com era, online commerce grew at an incredible rate. As a consequence, day trading became available to the entire public. It demonstrated to individuals that day trading, like other professions, is a job in which one can achieve by acquiring the appropriate information and skill set. Day trading involves buying and selling stocks or any other financial asset throughout the day. To accomplish so, they'll need a number of skills and tools, as well as a grasp of when to buy and sell stocks. Large financial institutions sprang out of nowhere and started day trading on behalf of their clients. Banking organizations started to open securities branches for the general public, where they taught their consumers how to trade effectively.

Day trading has increased in popularity as a technique of making money since then. If you want to be a successful day trader, you need know the following:

Stock market comprehension: As a day trader, you need have a basic grasp of stock markets. The most popular stocks and companies in the stock market should be known to you. They'll trade with more volume, which is important in day trading.

The following are the basic ideas of technical analysis: Unlike fundamental research, technical analysis forecasts how the market will move over a shorter timeframe, which is crucial information for day traders. If you want to make a living off of day trading, you'll need this skill set. Technical analysis and chart reading courses are widely accessible on the internet. Various universities also hold offline sessions to teach this. Any of them will teach you the principles of chart analysis as well as how to use day trading tools.

Money management skills: Stock trading, by definition, does not enable you to spend an unlimited amount of money. You must set aside a particular amount of money for your trading company and correctly manage that money before you begin. To evaluate if your trading company is flourishing or failing horribly, you need keep track of your losses and earnings at all times. There are several books available online regarding day trading money management. Reading a few famous ones will help you have a strong idea of how to manage your risk and return ratio.

Learn more about trading psychology: Day trading is harmed by emotions, and you must be aware of how to regulate your emotions when trading. Trading psychology books have been authored by several successful day traders. It's a good idea to read a few of them before you trade. Because no organization can operate only on emotion, you must be able to control your emotions before entering the trading arena, whether you profit or lose.

What Characterizes a Day Trader?

Day traders are technical traders. They trade based on chart readings and ignore other indicators like as profitability, P/E ratio, debt-to-equity ratio, and so on. A day trader's sole instrument for making money is technical charts. Day traders typically trade in a single session and close all open positions at the conclusion of the day, leaving no open positions for the next day. Swing traders are those that hold positions until the next trading session or overnight.

A day trader may use a number of time periods on technical charts to trade. These time limitations may range from one minute to five minutes, fifteen minutes, thirty minutes, forty-five minutes, one hour, four hours, and even weekly and monthly. If you want to know how a day trader may use weekly or monthly charts, you need first comprehend the distinctions. Day traders choose their trading strategy by examining charts and identifying the ideal time period for them. Many day traders may spend hours in front of their computers each day. Many day traders, on the other hand, only trade part-time because they are too preoccupied with other careers or jobs to dedicate much time to trading every day. These traders may use weekly or monthly charts to establish the price level at which they will buy or sell any asset in this situation. They wait patiently for that level to occur after making that choice, and only trade when it happens. There are many ways to set up an alert to tell you when a certain price threshold is reached. Clients may get stock price updates through SMS from brokerage platforms. The majority of charting software can also send out notifications when a certain stock price level is achieved. They save time and money by trading this way, which they may use toward other money-making activities like working a regular job or doing other tasks.

One more thing. Scalping is a kind of day trading that requires a lot of skill. Micro-trading is sometimes known as day trading since it focuses on a short timeframe (such as one minute or a few seconds) and trades for little profits. They increase the lot sizes so that even little profits might add up to a lot of money. Due to the short period, scalpers may trade many times during the day, sometimes up to 50 times. However, this is a high-risk trading method that requires extraordinary trading skills. It is possible to lose all of one's trading money in a single session if this is not done.

Day trading is the practice of buying and selling on the same day. Day traders, on the other hand, may keep their positions open for a longer period of time than scalpers. It might take anything from a few minutes to many hours. The Internet is full of publications that portray day trading in a positive light, causing you to believe that this trading strategy will make you rich fast. However, this trading strategy demands a significant amount of hard work, knowledge, razor-sharp attention, and patience, not to mention a substantial initial investment. When day trading, you must be completely focused; you cannot afford to be sidetracked by anything. Day trading may be perfect for you if you can commit to this level of attention and dedication.

Day trading is also known as intraday trading. This term better describes a day trader since it implies that buying and selling takes place in a single day.

Day traders may develop other trading methods such as momentum trading, positional trading, swing trading, and long-term trading. All of these trading tactics are specialized types of trading that aren't usually classified as day trading.

Chapter One

Day Trading Basics

Yes, the goal of day trading is to make money. While volatile stocks are good for day trading, keeping them overnight might expose you to large losses the following day. When day trading stocks overnight in the expectation of a massive price rebound the following day, it's better to incur little losses on day trades than enormous ones.

Even if you lose money, ending your trade at the end of the day might help you minimize your day trading losses. It's considerably better if you can profitably close positions! You don't think you'll be able to make more money if you wait till tomorrow. A flock of three birds in the wild is always preferable than a single bird in the hand.

It's also vital to distinguish between trading and investing. While trading is a sort of investment, ordinary investing is a buy-and-hold approach that pays out over months or years. Day trading takes just a few hours, and swing trading takes no more than a few months.

There are two types of positions: long and short.

When you acquire a financial security, you are taking a long position on it. When a trader says he or she is long 100 shares of Intel stock, it indicates the trader purchased and owns 100 shares.

Taking a long position in financial security is done with the intention of selling them at a greater price later. You sell the securities you hold to settle a long position.

When you sell a security without owning it, you take a short position. When a trader says he or she sold 100 shares of Intel stock short, it indicates the trader sold the stock in the hopes that the price would continue to fall, enabling him or her to repurchase it at a cheaper price. It's similar to purchasing cheap and selling high, only the "selling high" component happens first.

Why would you want to sell something you don't have in the first place?

To begin, consider why you should do it in the first place. And the solution is simple: take advantage of falling stock prices. It's essentially the reversal of the previously outlined standard trading approach of purchasing assets at low prices and selling them at higher ones. You may earn money even during market downturns by selling assets at high prices and then purchasing them back at cheaper prices later.

So, how are you going to go about it? You may borrow securities from your broker, sell them, repurchase them when prices decrease, and repay the assets you borrowed from them, depending on your broker and if you're eligible. You earn from the short sale in the process.

However, keep in mind that short selling, like long positions, has risks, including the possibility of prices increasing rather than declining. In this circumstance, you may also experience trading losses.

You may be wondering why brokers or exchanges would lend equities to clients for short selling instead of selling the shares themselves. That is a fantastic question. And the reality is that most brokers want to invest in stocks for the long run. Why?

Why take a chance on short-term trades in a down-trending market when they can earn money by simply lending it to customers who want to short sell for a fee? This is beneficial to everyone. Short-sellers may benefit even in low markets because long-term investors maintain their shares and profit.

Institutional Traders vs. Retail Traders

Retail traders, whether part-time or full-time, do not work for a company and do not handle other people's money. Only a tiny portion of the entire trading volume is controlled by these dealers.

Institutional traders such as hedge funds, mutual funds, and investment banks, on the other hand, employ advanced technology and participate in high-frequency trading.

Human engagement in the operations of investment firms is currently quite minimal. Institutional investors may be highly aggressive when backed by professional analysis and large quantities of money.

So, at this point, you may be asking how a beginner like you can compete with the greatest players.

Our advantage is that we have a lot of autonomy and freedom. The law mandates that institutional dealers trade. Individual traders, on the other hand, have complete freedom to trade or not deal in an unsettled market.

Regardless of the stock price, institutional traders should be active in the market and trade large amounts of stocks. Individual traders are allowed to wait for market opportunities and trade when they arise.

Unfortunately, most retail traders lack the information necessary to decide when to trade and when to wait. If you want to be successful at day trading, you must learn to manage your emotions and develop patience.

Losers' main issue in day trading isn't a lack of capital or technology; it's a lack of discipline. Many individuals have poor money management and engage in excessive trading.

The guerilla technique, which refers to an unconventional approach to trading influenced by guerrilla warfare, has shown to be helpful for certain retail traders. Guerilla combatants are competent at manipulating a more visible and less mobile conventional opponent using hit-and-run tactics such as raids, sabotage, and ambushes.

Keep in mind that your objective isn't to compete with institutional traders. Instead, concentrate on waiting for the greatest chance to get the funds you want.

Market volatility may benefit you as a retail trader. If the markets stay flat, it may be tough to earn money. Only institutional traders have the necessary abilities, expertise, and cash to gamble in such a situation.

You must understand how to choose stocks that will enable you to make rapid judgments on the downside or upward on a regular basis. High-frequency trading, on the other hand, is used by institutional traders to benefit from even little price swings.

In a nutshell, retail traders are on the lookout for Alpha Predators. These equities tend to fall when the markets are rising and rise when the markets are falling.

It's typically good when the market and the stocks are both going in the same direction. Simply ensure that you're trading shares that move for reasons other than market circumstances.

You may be wondering what kind of trigger stocks are ideal for day trading.

Reversal traders usually choose stocks that are trading down due to unfavorable news surrounding the firm. Many traders will notice and begin examining the stock for a bottom reversal when there is a significant sell-off due to poor news.

How do you figure out which stocks are popular among individual investors? There are a few tried and true methods for doing so.

Stock scanners for day trading are a fantastic place to start. Stocks that are going drastically up or down in price are of interest to retail traders.

Second, seek for retail-related social media groups or online communities. Twitter and Stock Twits are fantastic sources of current events information. If you follow successful traders on a regular basis, you can observe what they do. Joining a day trading community has various perks.

Securities are under consideration.

Many investors, traders, and analysts concentrate on market movements or indexes for a purpose. It's because they understand that, unless there's a compelling reason not to, most financial assets will follow the broad trend of their particular markets. When the Dow Jones rises, for example, most NYSE stocks rise with it, and vice versa.

Outliers, on the other hand, will always exist, who deviate from the overall trend for a special cause. Despite the fact that their total markets are shrinking, they are improving. Their stock prices are falling at the same time as the stock market is rising.

Securities in play refers to these securities (SIP). These are the securities you should concentrate on as a retail or individual day trader in your chosen day trading market.

If you want to day trade stocks, look for equities on the NYSE or NASDAQ that defy the overall trend. Futures contracts will be in contradiction to the majority of other comparable arrangements if they are used.

Do you understand what I'm saying? Right!

What are some of the possible causes of SIPs' irrational behavior? Unexpected profit results, corporate or economic occurrences, and significant government policy swings are just a few examples.

A security is not a SIP just because it deviates from the general market trend. The contrarian movement should have a reason. If there aren't any, it's most likely not a SIP.

Another key day trading guideline to remember, especially when selecting SIPs to day trade, is that: Determine if a security's movement is related to broad market sentiment or a specific underlying cause. This will need some research. As a rookie day trader, you may need to perform a little more research than usual. You'll be able to tell if a security is just following the overall market trend or is moving for a particular cause as your day trading expertise grows.

Day traders that make a livelihood doing this kind of trading are known as professional day traders. Day trading is sometimes dismissed as a fun pastime or a way to get a gambling high. You'll virtually certainly lose money if you don't grasp the market and its basics.

Consider yourself to be an expert.

When deviating from the script is acceptable: While it is true that a competent trader must adhere to their plan even when their emotions urge them to abandon it, this does not imply you must do so all of the time. Without a doubt, you will sometimes find yourself in a scenario when something outside your control renders your strategy useless. You must be sufficiently aware of your strategy's flaws, as well as changing market circumstances, to recognize when sticking to your predefined course of action will result in failure rather than success. Recognizing when a situation is improving and when your emotions are attempting to take over requires practice, but just being aware of the difference is a significant step forward.

Trades that are out-of-the-money should be avoided at all costs.

While a few methods prioritize acquiring options that are presently out of the money, they are the exception rather than the norm. Keep in mind that the options market is not the same as the stock market, which means that buying cheap and selling high is not a feasible strategy. If a call has gone out of the money, there is frequently less than a 10% chance that it will return to acceptable levels before expiry, meaning that buying these options is really gambling, and there are methods to gamble with chances far higher than 10% in your favor.

Keep your initial approach in mind, but don't become too attached to it: it's not the only method you'll ever need. Your primary trading strategy should fluctuate and adapt as the conditions around your trading habits change and develop. Additionally, you'll want to develop supplementary strategies that are more particularly geared to certain market conditions or unique tactics that are only applicable in a restricted number of scenarios outside of your core strategy. Keep in mind that the more prepared you are before beginning a trading day, the higher your total profit level will be.

Use the spread to your advantage.

If you're not completely risk averse, using a spread to protect your current assets while still generating a profit is the ideal approach to benefit from unexpectedly advantageous deals. Create two options: a call and a put, both with the same underlying asset, expiry date, and share size but two striking prices that are drastically different. The call will require a higher strike price to reflect the upper limit of your gains, while the put will need a lower strike price to reflect the lower limit of your losses. It's critical to acquire both halves of a spread at once, since doing so in fits and spurts might introduce additional components into the formula that are difficult to correct for. Never take anything without first determining market sentiment: While adopting a customized trading strategy is always the best option, it's still vital to gauge the market's mood before beginning the day's trades. To begin, remember that the collective desire of all present market participants is equally as powerful as something more specific, such as market news. Even if corporations offer positive news to several media channels but the news isn't as fantastic as everyone expected, related prices may fall.

You'll want to know the typical daily statistics that are regular for your market and be on the lookout for them to start lowering rapidly to get a genuine picture of how the market is now feeling. While a day or two of high volatility is expected, anything longer than that is cause for concern. Furthermore, you should constantly be informed of what your industry's main corporations are doing.

Even if the risks are minor, having a clear entry and exit strategy in place before to trading is critical. Finding your first set of entry/exit points without the help of a professional might be tough, but it is critical that you do it before you start trading. Starting without a solid understanding of the playing field may result in you losing your money unless you're really fortunate. If you're not sure what restrictions to establish, start with a generic pair of points and work your way down.

Setting up entry and exit points is important, but putting them to good use is much more important, especially if money is still on the table. One of the most difficult hurdles for new options traders to overcome is the belief that every good transaction should be exploited to the fullest extent possible. The fact is that as long as you have a lucrative trading technique in place, you will always have more profitable transactions in the future, which means you should be more concerned with safeguarding the profit that the trade has already created than with a modest extra profit. While you could earn a little more money if you ignore this advise every now and then, you're more likely to lose far more than you gain if profits rise and then plummet before you can pull the trigger appropriately. If you're still having trouble grasping this notion, consider the following: Trading options is a marathon, not a sprint, and the patient and steady always come out on top.

Never, ever give yourself another opportunity.

Many new options traders will find themselves in a situation where the best way to recoup a significant loss is to double down on the underlying stock at its most recent, significantly lower, price in the hopes of profiting on the assumption that things will turn around, and then continue to do so until everything is completely profitable once more. While it may be tough to let go of a once-profitable underlying stock, doubling down is almost never a sensible decision.

If you're wondering if the transaction you're about to make is a good one or not, consider whether you'd make the same decision if you were blind. The response should reveal all you need.

You'll need the guts to talk yourself down from the ledge and reduce your losses as much as possible given the present scenario if you find yourself in a position where doubling down seems to be the best option. If you cut your losses and move on from a failed deal as soon as possible, you may focus your attention and resources on a transaction that still has the potential to benefit you.

There is no need to take anything too seriously.

Humans have a natural drive to build connections with inanimate things of all kinds, including individual stocks and currency pairings. This is why it's completely natural to form a stronger bond with individual transactions and even contemplate abandoning your strategy if one of them fails. However, thinking about something and acting on it are two completely different things, which is why it's crucial to be aware of these inclinations and avoid them at all costs.

This situation occurs often, regardless of whether transactions are good or negative, and the outcomes are always the same. Because a transaction is doing well and showing no signs of slowing down, it may be tempting to leave it open for much longer than you would normally consider. In these situations, it's better to sell half of your stock and then establish a new goal based on the most current data to guarantee you have your cake and eat it too.

You're not taking your broker selections seriously.

With so many things to consider, it's easy to see why many beginner option traders just choose the first broker they find and start trading. However, the broker you select will have a significant influence on your whole trading experience, so choosing the proper one is critical if you want the greatest results. This implies that the first thing you should do is go underneath the attractive surface of their website to see what they have to offer. Remember that although designing an attractive website is simple, populating it with authentic material when you have bad purpose is far more difficult.

First and foremost, this entails looking into their customer service history to ensure that they not only treat their clients properly, but also that the quality of their service is up to pace. Remember that every second counts while negotiating a contract, so if you need to call your broker for assistance, you need to know that you'll be working with someone who can fix your issue swiftly. The easiest approach to see whether their customer service is up to par is to call them and see how long it takes for them to respond. If you have to wait more than one business day, you should consider going somewhere else; picture how bad the service will be after they get you where they want you.

Following that, you'll need to think about the costs that the broker will collect in return for their services. Shopping around will almost probably pay you since there is basically no control over these expenses. In addition to costs, account minimums and any fees associated with removing money from the account must be considered.

Look for a mentor.

When it comes to converting from a casual trader to someone who trades effectively on a daily basis, there's only so much you can learn on your own before you need an impartial eye to make sure you're on the right track. This individual might be someone you know in real life or someone you meet online. Finding another individual or two with whom you can bounce ideas and gain from their expertise is the key. Option trading does not have to be a one-time event; make advantage of all available resources.

Chapter Two

Account Opening

A trader must first open an account with a brokerage company in order to begin day trading. The trader must supply their name, address, and other personal information to the broker, among other things. All fees should be examined by the trader. These prices include the transaction commission as well as any other fees that may apply. In the case of Light Speed, if the account balance is less than US$15,000, the firm charges a US$25 monthly fee. If an account is dormant for a long length of time, some brokers charge a fee. Sure Trader, for example, charges $50 each quarter if fewer than 15 trades are performed in a given quarter. Brokers often demand extra fees for additional services. Speed Trade, for example, charges $60 for each international wire transfer. Some brokers have additional transaction criteria that must be completed. Consider the case below: If a trader employs Sure Trader as their broker and trades Penny Stocks24 with margin, Sure Trader may liquidate the trader's account.

Consider the case below: To engage in the stock market, a retail trader opens a day-trading account with a stockbroker. Assume that each transaction costs $5 and that each round trip costs $10, as indicated in the table below. To break even on an investment, a retail trader who buys one share of a corporation for $30 needs a positive price movement of US $10, or a cumulative effect of price movement and dividend payments of US $10. A price change of US$10, on the other hand, signifies a considerable 33 percent rise or reduction. To benefit on a smaller price shift, the trader must increase the number of deals he or she makes. To put it another way, they will need to buy several shares. Consider the case below: If a retail trader buys 5 shares at $30 each (for a total of $150 for the long order), the trader will break even with a positive price movement of just $2 per share.

When a retail trader engages in forex trading, he or she may seek to profit from interest rate swings (pips). A pip is a unit of measurement that represents how much the exchange rate of a currency pair has changed. Let's say the EUR/USD exchange rate moves from 1.2250 to 1.2251, or vice versa. A pip is 0.0001% of a percent fluctuation in the price. A pip is 1/10,000 of a dollar, or 1/10,000 of a dollar in other words.

There are various brokers in the forex market, just as there are in the stock market. Some of the most well-known forex brokers are Ameritrade, Ally Invest, ATC Brokers, Forex.com, FX Choice, and Oanda. FX Choice has a simple and cost-effective commission structure. You will be charged $0.09 each transaction factor if you use FX Choice. Furthermore, this cost is only collected when an order is completely fulfilled. For a trading factor of 0.05, the charge would be US$0.45, and the commission would be US$1.80 for a trading factor of 0.20, and so on. As a consequence, even if the gain per dollar is just a few cents, an individual retail trader may profit from forex trading. Retail traders who trade forex, for example, may trade with a smaller account and still make money, but retail traders who trade equities cannot.

It's worth mentioning that spreads for key currency pairs tend to swing between 7 and 9 basis points during regular trading hours on weekdays (for example, at 9:30 a.m. on Monday) (pips). To break even on a transaction, a retail trader's order would need to be 16 to 18 pips in the right place, depending on the cost of charge of US$0.09 per trading factor of 0.01.

The minimum account size is also important since traders who do not fulfill the minimum account size criterion will be unable to trade with that broker. Fidelity, for example, has a minimum account size of US$2,500 in order to trade equities. For forex trading, FX Choice requires a minimum account balance of US$100. It is significantly easier for a retail trader to enter the forex market than it is to enter the stock market because of the low minimum account size requirement and the small but proportional amount of fee charged.

The Financial Industry Regulatory Authority's (FINRA) rules are a major source of worry. Pattern day trading accounts must have a minimum equity of US$25,000, whereas non-pattern day trading accounts must have a minimum equity of US$25,000, according to the Financial Industry Regulatory Authority (FINRA). Because most day traders will make more than three round-trips over the course of five trading days, they will need an account balance of at least US$25,000 to participate in active trading activity. Sure Trader, a broker based in Nassau, Bahamas, claims that it does not follow the FINRA's PDT regulations. As a consequence, a trader with less than $25,000 in capital may use Sure Trader to engage in active stock trading.

The distinction between the financial criteria for trading equities and the financial criteria for trading foreign exchange is important to note. A retail trader may make a profit of $1 if there is a positive price movement of 118 pips (US 11.8 cents) and a trading factor of 0.01. In terms of the risk involved, if the market moved 100 pips in the incorrect direction, the trader would lose US$1.18. In the case of equities, however, a trader who buys 5 shares at $30 each and expects for a $2 price increase would have to risk $150 to break even.

When conducting transactions, it's also crucial to consider the broker's web platform. In the United States (US) and most exchanges in developed countries, for example, the broker would provide an online platform that enabled traders to execute trades immediately after placing orders. However, it is probable that there would be no online platform for trading in developing countries. The position for brokers trading on the TTSE market is as follows.

The absence of an internet platform provided by brokers inside a certain country causes an inefficient exchange. To place an order for a certain investment or commodity, a trader would often need to physically visit the broker, fill out some paperwork, and exchange currencies. The stock market may see only minor changes as a result of these situations. On rare days, there may be no transactions or price movement in specific firms, which is uncommon in the stock market.

Large spreads between the bid and ask prices are conceivable in markets. This may be a hurdle for a trader who desires to liquidate a large portion of their assets at once, since the trader may have difficulties finding buyers for his or her holdings. Traders may be obliged to accept a lower price for their assets than they would want as a result of this.

When it comes to stock exchanges in developed countries, Market Makers are often present to aid with liquidity. Market makers are those who buy and sell assets when no one else is willing to deal them. There may not be a Market Maker on the exchange in underdeveloped countries.

Please bear in mind that in order to open a trading account, all brokers will want the following information from the account holder:

two valid photo identity papers (driver's license, national identification card, passport); bank account information; employer's address and phone number; and financial information (annual income, and total net worth).

You may be required to complete additional requirements in order to open an account with some brokers. For example, Sure Trader needs the following: professional and financial references

Proof of address (e.g., a recent utility bill, bank statement, or other document indicating the account holder's address); and

Non-US people must submit a W-8BEN form, non-US organizations must submit a W-8BEN-E form, and accounts including both non-US entities and individuals must submit a W-9 form.

Before you start trading, ask yourself these important questions.

Before joining any market, an investor should ask himself or herself the following questions:

• What kind of financial markets are being considered when it comes to trading?

- In this scenario, what is the trading strategy?

- What factors are considered while picking stocks?

- What type of scanners and settings are used?

- What type of strategy should be employed? Price crossover and reversal trading methods, for example, are both instances of trading strategies.

- What are the statistical outcomes of their paper trading strategy?

- The time when the transaction was completed. What are the consequences of such dealings?

- What is your risk management strategy?

- What is the company's profit-to-loss ratio?

- What is the most you've ever lost in terms of money?

- Losses happen on a regular basis, but how often? What is the statistical likelihood of suffering a financial loss?

Stock markets, as previously stated, allow for the trading of stocks, whilst FX markets allow for the trading of currency pairs. In order to make educated judgments regarding their transactions, a retail trader in the stock market must analyze and assess the stock market's features. The trader makes money by selling stocks at a higher price than they were acquired for, plus the cost of the broker's commission.

In order to make educated trading choices in the forex markets, retail traders should focus their study on currency pairings and the elements that impact them. Forex trading is appealing because it allows regular traders with small accounts to trade on margin and profit on pip value changes. In the foreign exchange market, a pip is the smallest unit of change in the value of a currency pair. Assume the price of a currency pair increased from US$1.259 to US$1.260, as shown in this example. In the previous 24 hours, the price has moved by US$0.001, or one pip. 25 To conduct transactions with their brokers, forex traders might employ trading parameters linked to pip values. To decide how much of their cash is risked on each deal, retail traders employ a trading factor, which is similar to a betting scale. When utilizing a trading factor of 0.01, for example, just a little portion of a retail trader's account is at risk during a trading transaction. If the transaction is closed off at a trading factor of 0.01, the appropriate position of a trade for 10 pips would result in a profit of just 10 cents. A transaction in the right position for 10 pips would have resulted in a profit of US$1 if the trading factor was 0.10. With a trading factor of 1.00, a transaction in the suitable position of just 10 pips would have resulted in a profit of US$10 if the trade had been performed correctly. It should be remembered that, although increasing the trading factor may increase the payout of each successful transaction, it may also increase the loss of each unsuccessful transaction. As a consequence, if traders are not to see their account balance fast decline, they must be aware of how much money they are risking with each trading component.

Rookie traders should keep note of the tactics they employ, the times they use them, and the profits they achieve when paper trading. Traders should maintain meticulous records of their true profit/loss ratio. A profit-loss ratio of 2:1 or above is regarded good in business, as previously indicated. In other words, the strategy would be judged adequate even if the chosen technique resulted in a trader earning a profit 50% of the time and a loss 50% of the time. Furthermore, a higher profit to loss ratio indicates that a trader might make a lot of money despite making a lot of market blunders.

Retailers must also examine how they make real-time decisions when engaging with consumers. Because markets may move fast, traders who are slow to do research may miss out on lucrative opportunities. Traders should utilize the paper trading approach to familiarize themselves with their broker's trading interface. Paper trading may also be used by experienced traders to try out new trading strategies and earn vital experience.

Retail traders, like any other traders, need a strategy to manage their risks and losses. Consider the following scenario: the market takes a sudden turn for the worst. Before closing a position, the trader should decide how much loss they are ready to absorb. For example, if the price of an asset drops by 30 cents while the trader is maintaining a long position, the trader may choose to terminate the transaction to keep the loss from increasing.

For retail traders, risk management is critical. Consider the case below: A trader wins 15 consecutive transactions, but each time they win, they invest their whole profit in the following deal. Then, if they make a mistake and initiate a losing trade, they risk losing all they've earned. The trader would have a 15/16 (94 percent) success rate in this example, but since they failed to properly manage their risks, they would risk losing all of their profits on the one occasion when they failed to trade.

Traders should only use real money if they have a profitable trading strategy that has been tried and proven.

There are several classifications for orders.

The trader will need to place stock orders in order to participate in paper trading. In the financial sector, a trade order is an instruction to a broker from a trader or investor to enter or exit a market position. Trades may be entered in a number of different ways. Long orders are those that are placed to purchase an asset. Short orders are orders to sell a certain asset. The trader's expectations for the future of the stock market dictate the direction of the trader's order. They may place long orders if they believe the price of an item will rise, with the purpose of acquiring the asset and reselling it at a higher price. If they have stocks on hand and believe the price of those stocks will decline, they may place a short order. Short sellers may use a short order to short sell a stock if they believe the price will fall but do not own the stock.

Market, limit, stop, conditional, and duration orders are among the various types of orders available. The most prevalent are market orders.

You advise a broker to purchase or sell an asset at the current market price when you place a market order. If a trader issues a long market order, the broker will buy the asset at the asking price on the trader's behalf. Orders made on the market are often filled immediately. Market orders, on the other hand, have the disadvantage of not guaranteeing a price at which the order will be fulfilled. There may be some price slippage while market orders are fulfilled. Consider the case below: A trader used a market order to sell 1,000 shares of a stock they already owned. This order can only be fulfilled if the broker can find other traders interested in acquiring the stock. It's probable that the first purchase order will be for 500 shares at a price of US$20 per share. After then, a second order for 300 shares at $19 per share might be made. It's probable that a final order for 200 shares at $18 each may be issued. Despite the fact that all 1,000 shares were sold, the dealer paid $19.3 per share on average.

Restrict orders are used by certain traders to limit the amount of slippage they might encounter. A limit order defines how much of a certain item should be traded and at what price the asset should be traded. Unlike a market order, which requires the trader to buy an agreed-upon amount of an asset at the current market price, a limit order requires the trader to specify the quantity of the asset that must be bought at a certain price. Traders employ limit orders to safeguard themselves from price changes that are harmful to their holdings. A trader may, for example, issue a limit order to buy 1,000 shares at $20 in the hopes of profiting. This assures that the price of each share purchased is the same. If the stock price hits $26, a trader may use a limit order to sell 1,000 shares at or over $26. If the stock price increases to $25, the trader may issue a limit order to sell 1,000 shares.

A stop order is an instruction to purchase or sell an asset only when its price reaches a certain threshold. A long stop order is one that is placed above the current market price, while a short stop order is one that is placed below it. The order is promptly converted to a market or limit order whenever the asset's price reaches the stop level. As a consequence, stop orders are classed as stop market orders or stop limit orders.

A stop market order becomes a market order once the stop level is reached, and vice versa. When the stop level is reached, an order that was put up as a limit order will likewise become a limit order. It's natural to ask why any economic player would want a stop order to purchase assets at a higher price than the current market price. A trader, on the other hand, may use a stop long order to buy assets if their price increases over a certain threshold. A stop price might be set at a price that is perceived to be a resistance price by the trader. When prices break over resistance, it signals that the market is becoming bullish, and the trader may be able to benefit from the trend. Furthermore, if the stop price is at or below support in the event of a short-stop order, the market will have broken support once the market has hit the stop price. The trader would then be able to profit from the developing unfavorable trend.

Another kind of stop order that may be utilized in a number of scenarios is the trailing stop. A trailing stop order is one in which the stop limit is specified as a percentage of the current market price rather than the current price. The purpose of a trailing stop is to protect your gains as much as feasible. Trailing stops allow a position to remain open while prices are moving in the right direction, but they compel it to close if the price moves in the wrong direction by a specified percentage.

The following example will demonstrate how to use a trailing stop. Consider the following scenario: a trader went long and bought a $50 stock with a 15% trailing stop order. Assume for a minute that the stock price is still rising. Until the order is completed, it will be accessible. However, only minutes after achieving an all-time high of $80, the stock price drops 15% to $68. The stop order will then be activated at $68.00, resulting in the position being closed.

A trailing stop, unlike a stop order, monitors the price of the asset automatically and does not need human resetting. Consider still another scenario. Consider the following scenario: a trader chooses to short sell an asset at $40 and closes the transaction with a 5% trailing stop order. Assume the asset's price decreased 10% to $36, then rose 5% to $37.8 during the following 24 hours. When the price hits $37.8, the stop order will be triggered, and the transaction will be closed.

Conditional orders are orders that are automatically canceled or submitted if specific conditions are met. The two most prevalent types of conditional orders are order-cancel-order (OCO) and order-send-order (OSO) (OSO). A trader in OCO may place several orders at the same time. When one purchase is completely completed, however, all of the other orders are automatically canceled. A primary order that generates multiple subsidiary orders after the first order is completed is one of the most prevalent forms of OSO.

Duration orders are orders that specify the amount of time an order will remain on the market until it is canceled. They are used to place stock market orders. The trading platform of the broker will decide the duration of order periods. The duration might range from a few minutes to a whole day. Some brokers may work with you for an extended length of time.

How to Find and Trade Stocks to Make Money

Some novice traders start by picking stocks of well-known companies that they like, then placing a trading order. Popular stocks, on the other hand, are unlikely to see large price swings of more than 10% in a matter of minutes over the course of a single day. Stocks with such big price movements are usually beneath the radar and driven by breaking news.

As a consequence of breaking news, day traders generally focus their attention on firms that will experience a large amount of transactions and big price movements. The increased volume and price of equities trading on the market might be attributed to a catalyst32.

Stock scanners may be used to find stocks that fulfill the stated criteria.

Finviz is quite user-friendly in terms of interface design. The stocks with the highest price changes will be shown first on the main page. Users may look for particular stocks by ticker, check their chart information, and read up on the latest news about them. The company's Price Earnings (P/E) ratio, market capitalization, float, price and price change, sector, and other financial indicators are also available. Finviz's charts are very useful since they use a lot of moving averages and candlesticks. A trader may easily detect resistance, support, bearish and bullish trends, as well as reversals, using chart data. Traders who pay a monthly membership price of $24.96 may get Finviz intraday charts.

According to the criteria selected by the trader in the search results, Google Finance contains an interactive filter that can be used to stock shares. Among the key indicators are the price-to-earnings ratio (P/E ratio), market capitalization, and dividend yield. Other characteristics that a trader might use to personalize their search include the firm's valuation, dividends, financial ratios, operational metrics, stock metrics, and other pertinent information. You may also use Google Finance to keep up with the newest stock market news.

Another excellent free stock scanner is Yahoo Finance. A trader may sort stocks by the biggest price gainers and losers, as well as the biggest price movers. Yahoo Finance provides historical daily prices for stocks, bonds, currencies, benchmark indexes, commodities, mutual funds, and other financial instruments, as well as other financial instruments. Yahoo Finance may also be utilized to stay up to date on the newest financial news. A user may also create a portfolio on Yahoo Finance, which can be used to monitor specific assets and investments.

Market Watch provides an excellent and simple stock scanner that is easy to use. It may filter stocks according to their price, volume, P/E ratio, and market capitalization. Stocks that outperform a market index, outperform their 50-day or 200-day moving averages, and are traded on certain exchanges may all be sorted out using the scanner.

Stock Twits may be used to check back at prior stock prices as well as stay up to date on company news. Stock Twits users may also post blogs on stock prices and changes, as well as the causes for these changes and expected future price movements, among other things.

The tools section will go through all of the many tools that may be used to help you make an informed decision regarding a transaction.

To find possible purchases, some analysts may use a number of stock scanners. For example, some customers may use Yahoo Finance to locate stocks with considerable price movement, then use Finviz to corroborate their results by looking at daily stock charts.

Traders may find suitable stocks to trade by reading the newest news about the stocks, in addition to employing stock scanners. In actuality, this is an excellent time to begin trading after examining the economic calendar. Another good time to make a trade is during the reporting period. Bloomberg earnings releases will show when specific publicly traded companies will report their earnings. As a consequence, a trader may go to Bloomberg, figure out when the companies would report earnings, and then add these stocks to their watch list of stocks to track. The trader may take a long position if favorable news about a company and its management is released, and a short position if negative news about a company and its management is exposed.

Trade Ideas is a very powerful stock scanner. This approach allows for real-time pattern identification. After logging up and choosing from a choice of pre-configured scanning options, an investor may utilize the scanning settings to locate stocks with bearish, bullish, or neutral tendencies. For example, if a company is exhibiting a bull flag pattern, a trader may set the scanner to look for stocks that have gained 5% in the past hour and have varied by 1% in the last 15 minutes. A trader with a small account, on the other hand, would hunt for stocks with a price range of $3 to $15. Alternatively, a trader might seek for stocks with a market capitalization of less than $100 million and a 5 percent gain in value in the past 50 minutes. Alternatively, before the market starts, traders may use the scanner to find shares with a low float36 and at least 10% of the float that can be acquired using pre-market orders. A trader may employ as many different stock scanner setups as he or she wants at the same time.

Trade Ideas delivers chart windows and alert windows that stream and depict events as they happen in real time as a consequence of the parameters that have been selected. An Odds Marker is also included in Trade Ideas, which uses probability to assess the efficacy of the techniques submitted in real time. There is also a free chat room on Trade Ideas where you may meet new individuals.

Participants in the chat room may talk about trading strategies and potential assets to trade with other people. While Trade Ideas' services are not free (they cost $99 per month), they may be quite useful to busy day traders.

Any trader considering day trading with real money should read Trade Ideas. Traders who are practicing with paper money, on the other hand, may utilize free filters like Finviz, Google Finance, and Yahoo Finance to keep their costs down while learning how to trade properly.

Making a Watch-List is a straightforward procedure.

Day traders are interested in trading stocks that have significant price volatility. This kind of stock may be heavily traded and responding to current news. Before purchasing any stock, all traders should create a watch-list. In fact, a trader may use stock scanners to help them create a watch-list of a few stocks, and then do research on the stocks to determine the best entry position for the trade.

There are a variety of approaches that can be used to create a systematic watch-list. The following are a few examples:

- Top-Down Analysis;

- Fundamental Analysis; and

- Technical Analysis.

Top-Down Analysis.

To put it another way, Top-Down Analysis is a method in which investors/traders first seek for assets in broad categories before narrowing down their search criteria. An investor/trader could start by looking at marketplaces, then sectors, industries, and finally particular enterprises.

Top-Down Analysis is used to study the stock market and is based on the premise that strong markets are generated by companies whose stocks perform well. Following that, an investor or trader can look into a certain industry, eventually weeding out the strong companies.

Top-Down Analysis is a strategy in which a trader or investor studies the markets first. Markets may be studied using benchmark indexes. For example, a trader may examine the Standard and Poor's (S&P) 500 Index38 to get insight into the overall performance of US shares.

Investors often use market indices as a benchmark for a market's performance since it is difficult to track the performance of an entire market. The Standard and Poor's (S&P) 500 Index, for example, is frequently used to assess the performance of the US stock market. It is made up of 500 major US firms. There are other prominent indexes in addition to the Russell 2000 and the Dow Jones Industrial Average.

Markets may be segmented by industry, for example, into the energy, health, and information technology sectors. Industry branches may be further split into sub-branches. The health industry, for example, may be separated into several sub-industries, such as the pharmaceutical industry, hospitals, residential care facilities, medical equipment, and so on.

The trader may then go on to individual stocks of companies, which is the last level. Traders may benefit from bottom-up analysis as well. They might start with a small set of firms and compare their performance to that of their industry, sector, and market at this point.

Top-Down Analysis is very beneficial in the trading of commodities, futures, stocks, and options.

Fundamental Analysis.

Fundamental analysis is the process through which a trader or investor analyses a company's financial statements in order to assess its financial health and potential for growth. Investors want companies with strong financial performance as well as tremendous growth potential.

The trader uses Fundamental Analysis to try to figure out the following:

• Is the income of the firm rising year after year?

- Is the company profitable right now? Are these kind of profits/losses becoming more common?

- The company's performance outperforms its competitors in the same industry.

- Is the company in a position to repay its debts?

The investor would be particularly interested in the information included in the balance sheets, income statements, and cash flow statements. Using the balance sheet as a starting point, an investor may construct a wide range of ratios. Some of the most important ratios to consider are the Quick Ratio, Current Ratio, Debt/Equity Ratio, Days Sales Outstanding (DSO), Days Inventory Outstanding (DIO), Days Payable Outstanding (DPO), Cash Conversion Cycle, and Inventory Turnover Ratios.

The Quick Ratio and the Current Ratio are often known as Debt Ratios in finance. The Quick Ratio measures a company's ability to fulfill short-term debt obligations using its most readily accessible assets (like cash). The current ratio gauges a company's ability to meet short-term debt obligations when current assets surpass short-term debt commitments.

The Debt-to-Equity Ratio shows how a business has supported its operations throughout its existence. Investors are often put off by high debt-to-equity ratios because they imply that the firm may have trouble paying its debt in the long run.

The DSO, DIO, and DPO are three different sorts of activity ratios that assess how well a firm converts its inventory into cash. The DSO shows how soon a business may recover its accounts receivable balance. Businesses with low DSOs recover cash from accounts receivable in a short period of time, while businesses with high DSOs recover cash from accounts receivable over a longer period of time.

Technical Analysis.

The study of a stock's historical price as well as the volume of transactions it has produced is known as technical analysis. The usage of price charts is used in technical analysis. Technical Analysis, unlike Fundamental Analysis, believes that stock prices provide sufficient information. The application of demand and supply ideas to explain the movement of asset values is known as technical analysis. A rise in the demand for stocks in comparison to the supply of stocks, for example, should result in a rise in stock prices. Similarly, an increase in the supply of a particular stock may result in a reduction in the stock's price. It's worth noting that technical analysis may be used to trade equities, commodities, currencies, futures, and options. Technical analysis may also be used to identify price trends in other asset classes. Various methodologies are used to confirm trends and anticipate future trends. Participants in the market who feel they have recognized certain trends might then devise a plan to benefit from those trends.

Before going on to real-world trading with real money, inexperienced traders should first create a paper account and trade with virtual money. They will be able to trade after they are certain that they have created a strategy that has previously shown to be profitable. New traders are advised to use free stock scanners such as Finviz and Yahoo Finance, which are both accessible online, while hunting for attractive companies. The Trade Ideas platform, on the other hand, is recommended for real-money traders since it enables them to quickly choose stocks based on a wide range of financial and technical aspects. Investors and traders may use a variety of tactics to select stocks. Top-down analysis, fundamental analysis, and technical analysis are the three primary techniques (as opposed to a combination of these). Every kind of analysis has its own set of benefits and drawbacks. Technical analysis, on the other hand, will be the focus of this book due to its widespread use among traders and investors.

Chapter Three

What to Trade

Stocks are by far the most popular investment instrument. They are suitable for both new and seasoned investors. Let's have a look at how to choose and buy the right stocks.

Determine the scope of the business.

Your choice of industry should be based on your interests and previous experience. If you're learning about interior design, pay attention to furniture and home goods manufacturers, for example. If you like computer games, check into game developers and video card manufacturers. Because you will need to diversify your assets, it is advisable to choose various sectors rather than just one. You'll have a better grasp of companies that affect your personal or professional life.

Investigate the Businesses in the Selected Industry.

It's likely that dark horses are now beating recognized market leaders when comparing enterprises in the same industry. To do so, browse to the website of the exchange you're interested in (MICEX, NYSE, or NASDAQ) and go through the list of traded assets.

Naturally, being a shareholder in a large firm seems to be advantageous and safe. Second-tier players, on the other hand, can't be overlooked since their stock values might change at any time. Such gains may benefit shareholders. Make a list of companies about which you'd want to learn more. Each one has to be thoroughly studied.

Examine the company's profile.

Work your way through all of the company's information that is available. How far has it come? What was it like to go through the transformation? What effect did important events in the company's history have on its stock price? What are your plans for the future? The direction of a company's prior growth often has an impact on its future development. Pay special attention to profit and loss statements.

Pay attention not just to your accomplishments but also to your failures. It's crucial to know how the company handles difficulties and what's happening with its stock right now. This will aid you in determining your risks right away. Don't forget about liquidity: the company and the goods it develops should be liquid today and in the future.

Learn about the company's latest developments.

As a consequence of your investment, the company's initiatives have a direct influence on your profits. It might work in your favor if the company is preparing to launch a new product or has achieved a breakthrough. Everything fresh piques people's interest, which increases the likelihood of stock prices rising, but there is no assurance of quick returns. For example, a change in leadership may have both positive and bad implications for the company's operations and, as a result, its value. Do not expect firms to grow rapidly. The stock values of several of the world's most prominent companies are continuously rising.

Examine your company's and industry's dynamics.

Examine the company's and its industry's performance during the previous several years. If the growth rate is declining, or even worse, negative, this approach isn't worth it. Purchasing stocks at a period of fast development is like to boarding the last train.

The dynamics of such firms are frequently healthier and more predictable, and predictability always reduces risk. Determine if you're ready to be a stakeholder in a business with such a future based on financial data. Unfavorable events that are likely to occur should also be noted; this will help you assess the hazards and your attitude toward them more objectively.

Analyze the information.

You've already done some research if you haven't skipped any of the previous stages. You may now seek professional opinion and hear what they think about the firm you've chosen's future prospects. Large investing organizations often give their own recommendations. You may receive the opinions of well-known experts and seasoned investors on the internet (including on their personal pages on social networks). Because analysts are not psychics, they will not be able to predict the exact conclusion. A professional outside viewpoint, on the other hand, could be able to supply the needed information. In addition, competent analysts often have access to confidential material. You may see stats from previous years. This will help determine if prior forecasts were accurate.

Make a portfolio of investments.

Several of the businesses from the first list are eliminated after the rigorous review of the previous paragraphs. Some are in financial distress, while others are at the peak of their achievements, and so on. As a result, you'll be provided with a list of one, two, or even three market participants. According to a prior research, stocks of a company with superior prospects should be acquired. It is not necessary to concentrate on a particular company from a certain sector. You may buy shares in two or three rival firms and see which one performs better.

Try to diversify your portfolio by include equities from ten to twelve different companies, so that any losses in one asset are offset by gains in others. As previously said, you must make investments in a variety of sectors.

It is not difficult to invest in stocks and benefit from them, and the multi-stage approach should not be misconstrued. In this case, multi-stage does not likely complicate the method, but it does facilitate and improve the result. A good plan needs time and concentration: It requires you to be armed and have stocks. The most essential thing to keep in mind is that you spend your time and energy lowering risks and generating cash, which stimulates.

Investing in stocks, like any other investment, has risks. You will not be able to avoid these threats, no matter how clever you are. The easiest method to deal with these threats is to limit your exposure to them. You must first understand your risks before you can devise strategies to mitigate them. You must be aware of the many types of hazards as well as the factors that cause a risk to become a threat to your earning potential.

The Different Types of Risks

A risk is losing half or all of the investment's value. Some risks are directly tied to your stock investment and purchasing power, while others have an indirect influence. Any investment comes with risks, so don't let them prevent you from buying stocks.

Financial danger.

Financial risk is an issue for even the most well-established firms. The failure of a corporation to pay its investors is referred to as this risk. Keep in mind that when a company declares bankruptcy, creditors are paid first, then shareholders and investors. Shareholders are more likely to lose their investment value when a company declares bankruptcy.

Risk from Interest Rates

It's used to show how a rise in interest rates will affect an investment after it's been purchased. This kind of risk is often associated with investments that generate obligations or require investors to be paid interest. Bonds are a kind of investment that generates liabilities.Interest rate risk has an influence on a company's financial status, especially if it relies on debt instruments to raise funds.

Stock investments are affected by this risk. When a company issues bonds or other debt instruments and interest rates unexpectedly jump, its ability to pay may be jeopardized. Interest rates that are higher indicate greater interest payments. This means the company must pay its creditors before paying its shareholders. Stock prices may decline as a result, or dividend payments may be postponed.

When interest rates rise, stock investors, especially in the energy and banking industries, tend to liquidate their holdings. Instead of equities, these investors may want to invest in debt instruments. Expert investors diversify their portfolios to mitigate interest risk by investing in money market assets that perform well and profit even when interest rates are high.

Market Risk.

Market risk refers to the fluctuation of demand and supply in the market. When demand for a certain item is great and supply is limited, the price increases. When no one wants a stock, though, its value plummets. Market demand causes stock prices and values to grow and decrease. This is why stocks are a risky investment in the short run. The stock market is unpredictable due to the millions of people that purchase and sell equities every day. The price of a stock soars in a flash. The next minute, the price of the identical stock plummets since no one wants to buy it. Aside from demand, other factors such as the financial condition of the issuing firm, the political and legislative climate, and inflation may have impacted the price of a stock.

The idea is that you shouldn't invest in stocks if you don't know what you're doing. You might lose a lot of money because of your ignorance.

Inflationary Threat

A decline in an investor's purchasing power is referred to as inflation risk. You can't get the same product as you could a few years ago at the same price and quantity. A dollar could buy 10 candies five years ago, for example. A dollar today will bring you the same sort of sweets, but the quantity will be less. You may only be able to buy 5 or less today.

How does this risk affect your stock investment strategy? Assume you buy a stock that pays a 4% dividend yield and place the rest of your money in a bank account that pays 4% interest. In a sense, you are earning. Your original investment may be threatened if interest rates increase and the issuing firm's financial situation worsens. Your second investment is safe and will not be affected by interest rate increases. Because you put the rest in a bank, your money earns whatever interest the bank pays.

The rate of inflation, on the other hand, is about 5%. Your pay is below the rate of inflation. This means you're losing money on your bank investment.

Paying taxes is a risk.

Tax risk refers to the decrease in what you can get. Stock investing is intended to improve one's wealth. There is a tax when there is wealth. You must pay a portion of your tax debt. This means you'll need to be tax-savvy to avoid paying more in taxes than you earn.

Political peril.

When the government issues new rules and regulations, certain firms are affected. Others may even go bankrupt as a consequence of a law, while others may gain from the same legislation. In a caustic and unfair political atmosphere, businesses may die or thrive. Because political and governmental issues may harm a company's financial situation, having a basic awareness of how politics works in various countries is beneficial. In certain countries, businesses may become political targets.

Personal and emotional well-being are at risk.

Personal risk refers to your incapacity to increase your investment when an opportunity arises. This might also refer to your inability to continue an investment owing to a monetary shortage. The first scenario arises when you have the financial resources to invest but are unwilling to do so. It's also conceivable that you don't have the funds because you spent them for an unexpected expense. The second scenario arises when you do not have an emergency fund to pay unforeseen costs. The first thing you should do when starting to invest in stocks is to make sure you have an emergency fund. If you skip that step, you'll be more likely to encounter these issues in the future.

Emotional risk refers to your inability to control your emotions while determining whether to buy or sell a stock. Most of the time, many investors allow their emotions to take precedence over their rational thinking. You may be hungry for more or afraid of losing money when it comes to stock investing. These are serious emotions that you should learn to manage when it comes to stock trading.

How to Lower Your Chances

Although stock market investing comes with a number of dangers, avoiding them is straightforward and doable. It is a mistake to let these risks prevent you from investing. When deciding whether or not to invest, risk should not be your major concern.

Stop, collect data, and educate yourself.

Before investing in stocks, gather as much information as possible. Learn all there is to know about stock investing. You are more likely to make and pick lucrative investments if you have greater information. So what if it takes years for you to master even the most basic basics of stock investing?

The most important thing is to lower your risks of losing money on a venture you're unfamiliar with. Although the best teacher may have the most expertise, it does not imply you should not prepare for a battle. Even if a financial guru tells you otherwise, don't start buying stocks unless you're sure you're ready. Although financial counselors are experts in their field, they will not be the ones to lose money.

Always remember the principles anytime you feel prepared to fight. When it comes to stock investing, always remember to remain grounded and return to the basics. These basic concepts may help you achieve your goals without losing a lot of money.

Diversification.

This word relates to a stock investing mix-and-match technique. You don't concentrate on just one investment. Your portfolio is made up of short-, intermediate-, and long-term assets. The percentage fluctuates depending on how you invest. If you're a risk-takers, you'll invest the majority of your money in short- and intermediate-term assets. Long-term investments get a smaller share of the pie. If you're a conservative investor, you're undoubtedly investing a significant amount of your funds in long-term assets. Short- and intermediate-term investments make up a small percentage of the total.

Investing in a range of financial products is another way to diversify your portfolio. You should not invest all of your money into the stock market since it is volatile.

Chapter Four

The Watchlist

You'll need to make a trading watch list if you're a frequent day trader. Essentially, this is a list where you may track a set of firms' daily share prices over time. On trade days, it serves as a menu.

A trading watch list should comprise active equities that are set to trade based on fundamental and technical fresh triggers. It may be done on a piece of paper, a notebook, or even a spreadsheet. To assist you in creating a watch list, a variety of software packages and other resources are available. Some brokerage businesses may charge a fee or supply it for free.

Regardless of how many watchlists a trader has, there are two in particular that no active trader should deal with: a general watch list and a dynamic watch list. The wide one might comprise hundreds of equities known to the trader. Each trader should narrow down their general watch list and create an active stock watch list before the market opens each trading day. This watch list should include equities that the trader has been watching for days or weeks and which are poised to make a technical move. The active trading list, unlike the general list, should not include too many stocks. It should include a few ripe stocks that the trader is acquainted with. To put it another way, a general watch list may include equities that the trader has recently or previously acquired, but an active watch list should include companies that the trader is now contemplating purchasing. Assume you're a frequent trader who holds 10 positions on average at any given moment. Normally, you'll be keeping track of many stocks so that if one sells, you may replace it with another from your watch list. This may assist you in avoiding having too much money in your trading account at any one moment.

A watch list is useful for a variety of reasons. Let's imagine you've done your research and discovered a firm you believe is solid and has a lot of promise, but the stock price now seems to be excessive or overpriced. You decide to wait till a better moment to buy. The watch list will be used to keep track of the stock price and to generate charts for trend analysis. This will help you determine when is the optimum moment to buy that stock.

Creating an Active Stocks Trading Watch List

A stock is considered to be in play when it is popularly believed to be a takeover target. Because of their low volatility, day traders often trade stocks in play, which provide manageable risks and trading possibilities. When a company's trade results are excellent or terrible, its stock moves slowly and has just a little price change, regardless of whether it has low volatility. This might happen just a few times a year. Long-term gain investors will love these companies. Long-term investors like firms with solid prospects and modest share price movement in the correct direction, and they don't mind if the price doesn't fluctuate much intraday. Day traders, on the other hand, purchase and sell stocks during the stock market's opening hours and close their positions before the market closes. They may trade for a few minutes or an hour before exiting the market. As a result, they need a higher degree of involvement than investors. They need shares that move and cause price fluctuations in order for their transaction to be profitable. After deducting the costs of acquiring and selling shares, stockbrokers earn from such price discrepancies.

Furthermore, the number of equities in play is rather substantial. Day traders desire liquid shares and quick entry and exit opportunities. This implies that stock shares may be bought and sold on the spot. It may take a broker longer to complete a profitable buy or sell transaction when a stock has restricted liquidity. The trader and the broker are unable to agree on a price for buying or selling. This is a concern for day traders since it might be the difference between a lucrative and unsuccessful transaction. Day traders utilize the amount of shares exchanged each day to determine what they believe to be exceptional liquidity. The majority of traders just want a hundred thousand shares exchanged every day, while some may require a million.

In a single day, the stocks in play will shift. An average stock will trade in response to the firm's news, which is normally released early in the morning, and the price will change based on whether the news is good or negative.

Good news for traders may not necessarily make investors pleased. Some of the larger businesses, such as Apple, Amazon, and Facebook, have continually traded stocks, which day traders will monitor. This is due to the enormous number of transactions and shares transferred. A day trader will hunt for excellent trading chances and appropriate trading levels here.

Other websites provide free stock screening tools to assist traders in identifying equities that are moving quickly, intraday, or breaking out ahead of the market opening. Market Watch and Busy Stock are two examples of these sorts of websites. ADVFN creates breakout stocks and top rankings for popular UK stocks. They also offer applications like Seeking Alpha that provide you real-time access to news sources. CNN, BBC, Reuters, and Bloomberg are just a few of the news outlets that provide timely coverage of significant business events and breaking news. Stock twits, for example, provides up-to-the-minute, relevant news to day traders.

The terms float and market cap are often interchanged.

As a day trader, it's critical to comprehend the relationship between company size, risk, and possible reward. Such knowledge is critical as you establish the groundwork for long-term trading objectives. Using this data, you may create a well-balanced watch list with a variety of market capitalizations.

The "market cap" of a corporation refers to the total value of its assets. It refers to the total market value of the company's stock. Multiply the number of shares by the stock price to get a company's market cap.

If a corporation has $50 million in shares, each worth $20, its market capitalization is $10 billion. The importance of market capitalization is that it allows traders to compare and comprehend the size of various organizations. Market capitalization aids in determining the market value of various firms. It also reveals how a firm is viewed by the market and how much investors and traders are willing to pay for its shares.

Stocks with a significant market capitalization.

Their market capitalization is at least $10 billion. They are usually well-known businesses that provide high-quality products and services. They have a history of providing consistent dividends to their shareholders and have seen stable growth. Consumers throughout the country and even internationally know their brand names. At the establishment, they are key actors in their respective businesses. They are appropriate for cautious investors since they are less risky and have a lower potential for growth.

Stocks having a market capitalization of less than $1 billion.

Companies having a market capitalization of at least $2 billion and up to $10 billion are often evaluated. Their market capitalization ranges from $2 billion to $10 billion, in other words. They are well-established medium-sized businesses with room to expand. These businesses are experiencing or will soon be experiencing fast growth. They're striving to increase their market share and boost their competitive edge. This is a crucial stage in their development since it influences their capacity to reach their full potential. They are less risky than new firms when it comes to risk.

They have greater potential than blue-chip corporations in terms of potential since they are expected to expand until they achieve their maximum potential.

Small Caps.

Their estimated market worth is between $300 million and $2 billion. They aid in the establishment of new enterprises in the sector. They're the most aggressive and risky, relying on specialty marketing to stay afloat in the market. They are sensitive to economic shocks due to their low resources. They face fierce competition as well as market changes. They are great for investors who can endure significant stock price fluctuations in the near term since they are young firms with huge long-term growth potential.

On the other hand, the float refers to the quantity of shares that are accessible for public trade. Free-float does not include locked-in shares, unlike market cap, which represents the entire stock worth of all firm shares. Employees and the government are the only people who can buy locked-in shares. A lot of things impact market capitalization. The market cap may be affected by a major shift in the value of shares, either upwards or downwards. The market capitalization fluctuates as the number of issued shares changes. As warrants on the company's stock are exercised, the number of shares outstanding increases, lowering the market valuation. This is because such an exercise is often conducted below the current market price of the shares, allowing it to impact the market cap. A dividend or stock split, on the other hand, usually has minimal influence on the market cap.

A trader's time horizon, risk tolerance, and financial objectives must all be considered while creating a continual watch list that includes large-cap, mid-cap, and small-cap stocks. A well-balanced watch list that includes companies from different market sizes might help you lower your investment risk.

There are pauses before the market opens.

Every trading day, between the hours of 8 a.m. and 9:30 a.m. EST, pre-market trading takes place. This normally occurs before to the start of the main trading session. While waiting for the normal trading session, traders and investors utilize the pre-market trading time to gauge the market's direction and strength. Liquidity and volume are limited during pre-market activities. During the pre-market time, large bid-ask spreads are prevalent. Although many retail brokers enable pre-market trading, the types of orders available are restricted. Direct-access brokers began offering access to pre-market activity as early as 4 a.m. It's critical to remember that the pre-market hour is quite calm.

Gapper and dumper stocks are the most dependable sorts of equities to trade during pre-market movement. They're frequently feasible during the time of the year when the results of numerous firms are released. These stocks may gap up or down with volume during such a season. A significant catalyst, such as press releases, news, or financial figures, frequently sets them off. They might be responding to rumors, analyst upgrades or downgrades, or a mix of both. When equities rise sharply in response to earnings releases and guidance, they gain increased 'tradability,' follow-through, and consistent volume. When trading before the market opens, keep in mind that there are fewer players, a bigger spread, and less liquidity. Trading pre-market is not recommended unless there is a large volume gap caused by a catalyst. For most traders, waiting for the market to open is the best choice.

Given the many advantages of day trading, it's difficult to understand why the majority of day traders fail. Why do the majority of these traders fail despite the fact that the activity seems to be lucrative? Understanding why traders fail might help you recognize the typical flaws that result in losses. As a result, you'll be able to trade more successfully since you won't make as many errors. The following are some of the reasons why traders lose money.

Constantly reliant on chance.

Assume Danny is a brand-new dealer in town. Danny has some market expertise since he is usually watching the news, particularly the stock market news. Danny, on the other hand, has never done business before. He believes he can attempt day trading since he knows the fundamentals. Danny has never written down any stock trading methods he could use. So, without thinking, he creates an account and purchases 400 shares.

During his lunch hour, the stock market rises, which is beneficial for him. Danny chooses to sell his stock after lunch. On his first transaction, he realizes a profit of $100. His second effort netted him $100 as well. Danny now believes he is a seasoned businessperson. He was able to make $200 in only one day.

Danny's day trading activity is likely to be short-lived, according to an experienced trader's appraisal of his position. Danny risks losing money if he gets the impression that his ideas are succeeding. He could be tempted to expand his stock ownership because he believes he would benefit. It's important to note that none of Danny's plans have ever been put to the test. As a result, his trading activities are not certain to be profitable in the long run.

Danny's problem is that he believes in his well-considered but unproven ideas. As a result, he may neglect trade tactics that may have kept him from making typical errors. Finally, he will be upset if he loses money, claiming that day trading is not profitable. This is where the majority of novices wind up. Their early success in online trading has blinded them to the need for more training. The plan has been abandoned.

Assuming Danny improves his trading after learning from his failures in the future. He presently uses a day trading method that has helped him for the last year or so. Danny believes he has discovered the finest path for him right now. However, there is a second issue to consider. Danny realizes that his strategy has failed him six times. He's caught in a bind, unsure what to do since he can't afford to keep losing money.

What does Danny really do? He approaches things differently. Danny believes it is time to attempt something new, regardless of how successful his prior method was. He should preferably use a novel and untested approach. It's vital to keep in mind that Danny is using an untested strategy. He is abandoning a tactic that has served him well for the last two years. Danny runs the danger of ending up back where he began. As a result of his decision to forsake his approach, he may lose money.

You should be aware that, although unpredictability may lead to gains, it can also lead to losses for traders. A trader must have a strong strategy that they stick to in order to prevent such volatility. This is a trading strategy that will lead them to success. Their arrival and departure plans should be well-documented. To assist a trader in making wise financial decisions, the plan should incorporate a money management approach.

Successful Trader Characteristics

Anyone may become a day trader, but you must adapt to the industry's expectations over time to survive in this highly competitive sector. As a day trader, you'll need to cultivate a variety of characteristics that will help you stand out from the crowd and stay afloat. Consider the following traits of effective traders:

They acknowledge and take full responsibility.

Good traders accept their losses without praising or criticizing particular individuals or situations. They correct their errors and go about their business as normal. Successful traders follow a formula.

They are steadfast in their belief in their trading strategy. Many successful traders are prepared to accept blame for their gains, but few are willing to accept blame for their losses.

There is no mention of the market-maker or broker, the market's odd behavior, the system, their risk management, or their ideas influencing their winning trade. During a loss, on the other hand, these stumbling blocks swiftly rise to the front of their minds. It's easy to blame someone other than yourself, the one who pressed the buttons, when things go wrong.

A feeling of duty at a gut level does not separate winners from losers. It is the same person. They all sprang from the same common denominator in this case: you. Will you use your accomplishment to boost your ego, or will you build on your achievements? Trading serves as a mirror to oneself, allowing one to see what needs to be altered and worked on, as well as expand on what is already working. And your weakest trading ability determines how much money you make and how successful you are. Talent, fortunately, is a drill that can be readily moulded into the foundation of your success.

They're really patient.

The majority of positions are known to successful traders as soon as they are opened. They'll have to wait in line. They have the patience to deal with trade uncertainties. Most traders develop a strategy to aid them in determining when and where to trade. If properly traded, such a technique should provide a profit. It may seem apparent, but traders have a problem: their minds get tricked into believing they're making a deal before the market structure has completely developed when they look at a fast-moving chart in person. You join early in order to prevent losing out on a good offer, but you usually lose.

Wait for the ideal opportunity to make your buy. You must also be willing to pass up opportunities; only choose transactions that will provide you the best setup and enable you to finish your transaction. Deals should only be made if the market requires it.

If you're following your method but still going into it too early, have a brainstorming session about what you might do better. Before you decide to join, wait for the price to reduce if it is now higher. Look for little signals that the price may climb again when it begins to swing sideways. If the trend continues, it could be better to hold off on entering the trade until the price reaches a high point. If the market wiggles during the retreat, look for minor price changes that indicate greater highs and lower lows.

These oscillations indicate that buying pressure will increase once again. When the price seems to be moving in the other way before shifting in the expected direction, you wait for it to happen before acting. Do not trade until you are positive it is the right moment. To earn money, you don't have to catch every large price shift. You are missing a step if you miss it.

Be patient; the market moves slower than we may anticipate. You'll be able to capture more of the price movements you're searching for and avoid wasting money on missed transactions if you wait for the correct setup and trigger.

They consider the future.

Day traders who are successful cannot get caught up in the past. Day traders need to be able to use historical data to make trading choices, but they also need to be able to use the data in real time. Traders are also planning their next movements, determining what to do based on the market's trend.

The markets are never static. We can't make a five-minute decision to acquire something at a certain price and then forget about everything that happened in the market during that time. Day traders are constantly considering their next move, which is dependent on fresh market data that arrives every second. They evaluate a variety of situations and plan how they will implement their trading strategy in each.

They don't engage in a lot of business.

Overtrading is the practice of buying or selling financial assets for no reason. To put it another way, taking on too many open positions or spending too much money in a single transaction. Individual traders are not protected by any rules or regulations regarding overtrading, although it may harm your portfolio. If trading brokers, who are regulated businesses, engage in excessive trading, they may suffer severe consequences. Overtrading should be avoided at all costs, and a thorough trading and risk management plan should be implemented. Stop emotional trading by understanding and arguing the differences between rational and emotional trading judgments.

If you have a lot of open positions, divide your money across multiple asset classes to assist decrease risk. Determine how much you want to risk with what you have, but never trade with more money than you can afford to lose. Overtrading should be avoided by experienced traders. They are aware that excessive trading puts their account at risk, but not everyone is aware that it is trading day. They're preparing for a difficult opponent.

They're flexible.

Traders that are successful are able to adjust to shifting conditions. They tailor their trading strategies and market-moving judgments to their specific needs. Successful traders are aware of their own trading personality.

They do not push themselves to change approaches or strategies since it is not in their nature. After a month of trading, you are allowed to make minor changes to your trading plan based on what you learned from your trading plan review sessions. Before being evaluated, trades focusing on these small strategic improvements should be undertaken for another month. Make no modifications to the strategy before the one-month mark since it is easier to make improvements based on individual transactions than than overall outcomes.

The difficulties that surface in your self-evaluation are handled on a daily basis. All you have to do for the self-evaluation is stick to your trading strategy, whatever it is. Your company will expand as the trading plan evolves, but it is always your responsibility to stick to the strategy. Your trading approach does not alter as a result of your daily self-assessment; rather, you improve your personality qualities in order to stick to the plan. Weekly, make little adjustments to your trading plan. The same principle applies to your daily self-evaluation. Your emphasis should be on one task at a time. When you try to cope with many problems at once, your attention becomes too spread out, and you are unable to focus on each one adequately.

Successful traders are those who take action. They don't allow their worries about their decisions control them or get in the way of their job. They've established efficient systems. Commercialization and analytics include high-probability, excellent trades, money management, avoiding tying in their strategies curve, and implementing their program into their company objectives. It is insufficient to just watch movies or read books. Before being adequately motivated to make trading judgments in ever-changing market circumstances, day traders must regularly practice what they are learning.

It's not only a case of putting forth the effort. You may day trade for years, putting in hundreds or thousands of hours, and yet make no progress since you are not focused on a certain activity.

To practice effectively, focus on a single task.

At this moment, the desire to trade comes into play. A trading strategy describes how, why, and when a trader joins and exits transactions, as well as how risk and position size are handled. It also determines when and which markets will be traded. The strategy comprises creating a plan that enables for monitoring of progress.

In a demo account, practice day trading one component of the trading technique at a time until the process becomes second nature. Charts, for example, might be used to choose entry points for your approach. Continue doing so until you've discovered all of the entrance points for your plan. Day trading requires quick reactions and precise precision. Practice so that entry happen when they're intended to, based on the approach. After that, the stop-loss must be changed. After that, try pinpointing your revenue target with pinpoint accuracy. Practice utilizing the correct position size for each trade, as well as the trading method's other trading components. While it may seem strange, you are always learning what not to do.

When conditions are good and your trading plan permits it, your goal is to develop the habit of not only following your strategy and executing all of the trades you're directed to execute, but also of sitting on your hands when your strategy doesn't. It's just as important to avoid making agreements as it is to make them. Your plan should not be adopted unless it creates a trade incentive. The patience required to wait for a suitable trade signal is lacking in most beginning traders, but it can be mastered with experience.

Practice being careful and seizing legitimate trading chances. Each aspect of a trader's trading strategy will be given different levels of attention. Each component of the trading strategy will typically take 15 to 20 days to complete. If a trader employs this approach, after around six months of experience and clear comprehension of how to apply it in all market conditions, they should have a full grasp of their trading plan.

They have good manners.

To be successful, every trader need discipline. The market provides almost endless trading opportunities. Thousands of different items are exchanged every second of the day, yet just a handful of those seconds give enormous economic opportunity. If a strategy generates four to five transactions per day, stop loss and profit targets are automatically set for each transaction. There are just around five seconds of serious trade activity per day.

Chapter Five

Strategies for Trading

Trading is more than just choosing stocks at random to keep or sell long or short. To gain money from their trading activity, the bulk of successful economic agents rely on a trading strategy. In truth, without a disciplined approach to trading, it is difficult for any trader to consistently produce gains over time.

There are several trading tactics available in the realm of trading. Some trading strategies are simple enough that even rookie traders can utilize them. The employment of technological software and technology demonstrates the complexity of other approaches.

This chapter covers a variety of basic trading procedures that may all be used by the average economic actor.

It's a set of rules that traders use to determine when to enter and leave deals. The following is an example of a trading strategy: Both trade filters and triggers are used in the execution of trading systems. A trade filter is a set of criteria that must be met before an asset is added to a trader's watch list and considered for a transaction. A trade trigger is a date and time stamp that specifies when a transaction will be processed.

All trading systems should have rules for entry, exit, risk management, and position size. All trading strategy should incorporate regulations. The points at which the trader has decided to enter deals are known as entries. They may be sorted based on a number of factors. For example, when the market is open, a trader may establish an entry position at the open price and an exit position at the close price. If a chart pattern is validated, the trader may choose an entry position as the first or second candlestick that is consistent with the found pattern.

Exits may identify positions that would finish a successful trade after a specified profit has been attained, or they can define positions that would minimize a loss. Every trading technique has some risk, since there is always the possibility of a market player losing money. Trading tactics that decrease the amount of money lost when losses do occur are the most successful. This does not rule out the possibility of total eradication. Instead, it allows the trader to cut their losses early and move on to the next transaction. The quantity of stock or futures contracts that a market participant is prepared to risk with each transaction is referred to as position size. The size of the trading capital owned by the market participant in question determines this. As the table above shows, transactions with larger trading capital are nearly always more lucrative than deals with lower trading capital.

Apart from the basic rules, trading tactics may be divided into other categories. Crossovers, momentum, volatility breakouts, reversals, event trading, and Heikin-Ashi are just a few of the various types of trading strategies accessible.

Crossovers.

A crossover is a basic trading strategy based on an asset's price or moving average shifting from one side of a longer moving average to the other side of the longer moving average, rather than the opposite side of a shorter moving average. Price crossover strategies and moving average crossover strategies are the two types of crossover trading approaches.

When the price of an asset goes above (or falls below) its moving average, it is said to have crossed over (or below). Consider the instance where an asset's price was initially lower than its 5-day moving average. This is a gloomy circumstance, according to experts. When the price of an asset suddenly rises and above its 5-day moving average, the price crossing technique is used.

A Moving Average Crossover occurs when an asset's moving average crosses over another moving average of a greater period. Consider the case where an asset's 5-day moving average was initially lower than the asset's 10-day moving average. Now imagine that the asset's price rises considerably, causing the 5-day moving average to grow in value. A moving average crossover occurs when the 5-day moving average exceeds the 10-day moving average at any given period.

Traders use crossovers to spot changes in the direction of a trend. They may be used to see whether an asset's price is breaking through barrier or support, indicating the start of a new uptrend or downtrend. Price crossovers will occur more often than moving average crossovers. However, they have the ability to provide traders false information. Because support and resistance levels may not be broken, traders seeking for breakouts utilizing Price Crossover methods may identify false trends. While assets with high volatility may often cross over short moving averages, this does not necessarily imply the start of an upward or negative trend in the asset's price.

Bullish and bearish crossovers are also possible. When the price (or short Moving Average) climbs above the Moving Average for an extended length of time, this is known as a bullish crossing (or longer Moving Average). It denotes the start of an upward trend. Long positions in the market may be taken by traders or investors. A golden cross represents a bullish crossing. It occurs when the 50-day Moving Average, a technical indicator, exceeds the long-term 200-day average.

A Bearish Crossover occurs when the price (or short moving average) goes below the Moving Average in technical analysis (or longer Moving Average). A bearish crossover signals the start of a downward trend. Traders or investors may elect to liquidate their previously held long positions or shorten their positions. A death cross represents a bearish crossing. When the short-term moving average (50-day moving average) goes below the long-term moving average, it is said to be bearish (200-day moving average).

Traders and investors often use several moving averages to detect trend shifts. An investor may use this information to make a judgment if a 50-day moving average crosses a 100-day moving average, as well as a 50-day moving average crossing a 200-day moving average. It's worth noting that the later Moving Average Crossover Strategy would act as a trend indicator since a trend must emerge before the moving average crossover can happen. Furthermore, lengthier Moving Average Crossovers are better predictors of long-term trends than shorter Moving Average Crossovers. Crossovers are more reliable short-term trend predictions than other indicators.

Long-length moving average crossover strategies would be of interest to an investor who is worried about the market's long-term future. These traders use moving average crossover methods that are slow to react to short-term price swings in the market. An investor would be interested in the crossing of two Moving Averages, such as a 50-day Moving Average crossing a 200-day Moving Average or a 100-day Moving Average crossing a 200-day Moving Average.

Day traders might be interested in moving averages with a limited time horizon. Crossovers such as a 5-minute moving average crossing over a 10-minute moving average and a 10-minute moving average crossing over a 15-minute moving average may be employed in day trading. Traders may use this to get short-term indications on whether to join or leave positions.

There is no such thing as an ideal length for a moving average. A trader's or investor's choice and usage of a moving average is dictated by their trading strategy, risk aversion, and the length of time they wish to maintain the asset in question.

Traders and investors may utilize filters in addition to crossings to confirm patterns and decide whether to join or quit a trading session. For example, an investor who wants to trade a 10-day Moving Average crossing over a 50-day Moving Average would wait until the 10-day Moving Average is at least 10% higher than the 50-day Moving Average before making a trade. The crossover is evaluated with the filter, and the quantity of erroneous signals created is reduced. Filters have the drawback of detecting trends after they have happened, which means that the investor may lose out on a portion of their potential gains.

Although the Simple Moving Average Crossover was used in the preceding examples in this section, a trader may want to use Exponentially Weighted Moving Averages for their crossover strategy. To select the kind of Moving Average to use, the trader must first assess his or her tolerance for false signals.

Bollinger Bands and Moving Average Envelopes are two common technical indicators.

Moving Average Envelopes are a kind of trading technique that uses moving averages as a trading approach. Establishing a confidence interval (for example, a 10% confidence interval) around a medium-term moving average is required to discover support and resistance levels (for example, a 25-day moving average). If the price of the asset fluctuates beyond this 5% confidence level, an investor or trader will get signals. Consider the case below: An asset's price dropped below 10% of its 25-day moving average. This tells the investor that the asset's price has broken through support and is likely to fall further in the near future.

A Bollinger Band may be used in addition to or instead of the moving average envelope. If the asset's price rises above one standard deviation from its moving average, it suggests to the investor that the asset's price has broken past resistance and that an uptrend is begun. The investor or trader may then choose to take a long position in the asset.

Momentum.

Momentum trading refers to when traders trade shares that are moving rapidly in one direction on a large volume. Before adopting a position that would allow them to produce a profit, an investor uses technical analysis to assess the market's overall direction. When a trader observes a bullish trend, he or she will take a long position to take advantage of the momentum. Furthermore, if the trader establishes a negative trend, they will short sell the stock to counter their losses and profit later in the trading cycle.

To fulfill the trading condition, the stock price must break through either resistance or support. To begin, the stock should be trading at a very high volume of transactions. An upward breakout in the market may be identified by a stock price trading at a new high. Similarly, a new low in stock price might indicate a bearish breakout in the stock market. To optimize earnings, advanced traders might employ econometric methodologies or computer tools to establish support and resistance levels, as well as breakouts. Those advanced methods, on the other hand, are beyond the scope of this project. This book is for rookie traders who wish to expand their expertise via trial and error.

Alternatively, a trader might create their own set of rules to improve the efficiency of momentum trading. To establish a long position in a particular firm, a trader may need the most recent candlestick to breakout and set a new high above the preceding 'N' candlesticks. If the value of 'N' is set to 5, the trader will get a buy signal on his or her

computer screen once the last candlestick has broken the high of the previous 5 candlesticks.

A trader's need that the second candlestick move outside of the Bollinger Bands before producing a signal is another example of conditions for establishing a buy signal. Because the majority of stock price movement occurs inside the Bollinger Bands, any movement outside of the bands may be interpreted as a price breakout.

Third, in order to make a good transaction, a trader may need that the latest candlestick increase by at least 'X' percent of the preceding "N" candlesticks, and that the high of the last candlestick be larger than the high of the prior 2N bars. A trader may start a long position if the latest closed candlestick increases by more than 0.5 percent over the previous three closed candlesticks and the high of the last closed candlestick is higher than the highs of the preceding six bars. The trader may try multiple values for 'X' and 'N,' and then choose the alternatives that produce the most successful trades based on his or her tests.

It's feasible that increases in trading volume will also help the previously mentioned trade rules succeed. In order to benefit, the trader may require a rise in trading volume of at least 'X' percent in addition to stock price variations. In order to justify the return of momentum, the trader can need a relative volume of at least 2. This technique makes sense because when new trends arise, trade volume should rise in tandem.

Day traders are looking for parabolic movements as well. An exponential move in the price of a stock is known as a parabolic move (either a rise or a drop). It is conceivable for a stock to exhibit parabolic leaps as a consequence of its response to news. Stock prices should rise in response to good news regarding a company's sales and profitability. Negative news concerning a company's profitability or public relations is more likely to cause its stock price to drop.

Breakouts in volatility.

A Volatility Breakout is a trading strategy based on trading both upside and downside breakouts. A breakout is based on the premise that the market will break through resistance or support when it moves by a certain amount.

A trader's strategy should contain parameters that must be completed before a trade is designated as open in order to benefit from a breakout. For example, to go long, the trader may require at least three (3) 5-minute candles to break resistance, as well as a relative volume more than two (2). The solution might additionally contain a restriction for position size (say, 5% of total equity) and a rule for abandoning the transaction (perhaps closing the order after on the first 1- minute candle to make a pullback after achieving at least a 15 percent gain).

Volatility Breakouts, like other trading systems, have the power to create profits or losses. If a trader believes that indications are deceptive, he or she may lose money. A trader may join the market long and profit if a 1-minute candle rises 10% above resistance and is mistook for a breakthrough. A reversal of the item's price, on the other hand, is possible. As a consequence of going long, the trader took the wrong position and might lose a lot of money.

Because false signals are possible, traders may opt to utilize delayed indicators to identify breakouts in order to avoid obtaining erroneous signals in the future. To validate the pattern, an Exponentially Weighted Moving Average, for example, may be necessary to break both resistance and support. Using delayed signals has the drawback of confirming a pattern after it has already concluded, denying the trader the opportunity to execute a winning transaction.

Reversals.

The notion of trading reversals is crucial to a reverse trading strategy. The trader uses technical analysis to identify market reversals and then execute the appropriate transaction.

The Relative Strength Index (RSI) is a useful tool for spotting market reversals. Furthermore, as previously said, when the RSI exceeds 80, the stock is considered overbought. This might indicate that the trader's position is about to reverse. As a consequence, the trader using the reversal strategy may choose to short sell the asset. Similarly, a stock with an RSI of less than 20 is considered oversold. Using the opposite strategy, a trader would purchase the item and then sell it later.

When trading a reversal, cautious traders may opt to set their own tougher criteria. The RSI may be utilized to assess whether or not to go long, as well as whether or not to go short. A trader can supplement this by looking for at least one candlestick to reverse after about three consecutive 5-minute candlesticks of the same color have hit resistance or support, which can be done by looking for at least one candlestick to reverse after about three consecutive 5-minute candlesticks of the same color have hit resistance or support. When trading reversals, the trader should try to catch the stock as close to resistance or support as possible to maximize profit margins.

Trading in life's happenings.

News concerning a company's financial health, profitability, operational concerns, and scandals may all affect stock prices. The stock price of a company may be influenced by macroeconomic news that affects the company's financial health.

Currency pairs, for example, have a propensity to react to key economic news in the forex market. While the major currency pairs react to the bulk of economic news from developed and key countries, the United States is the most influential and closely watched news source (Bauwens et al. 2005; Roache et al. 2010; Lahaye et al. 2011). Because the United States has the world's largest economy and the US Dollar is the world's reserve currency, this is the case. This means that the US Dollar is used in the great majority of international transactions.

Data about the US economy, such as GDP growth, inflation rate, and the Federal Reserve's (Central Bank's) repo rate, may all influence market speculation and the level to which the US swings in comparison to other countries. Furthermore, news regarding international events such as war, natural disasters, political unrest, and presidential elections may influence dollar speculation.

For instance, the seasonally adjusted unemployment rate in the United States in May 2007 was 4.4 percent. When the global financial crisis and ensuing economic recession hit the United States, the jobless rate quickly climbed to a record high of 10% by October 2009. (US BLS 2018). The increase in unemployment coincided with the drop in the value of the US dollar. As a consequence, the US dollar's depreciation against a number of major currencies over the time period in question was unsurprising.

A retail trader who wishes to focus on news may do so by waiting for a period of consolidation prior to the release of normal economic news and then trading on the breakout of that consolidation. Because of the nature of news-based trading, positions may be held for a short time (as in intraday trading) or for many days (as in swing trading).

Financial assets (stock prices and currency pair prices) increase in value when good news is received, whereas financial assets (stock prices and currency pair prices) decrease in value when bad news is received. In the case of stocks, this happens as a consequence of a large number of traders being long on a specific asset after favorable news, increased demand, and a price rise. Negative news, on the other hand, causes traders to respond by closing long positions or short selling, resulting in a drop in demand and a drop in stock price.

The word "event trading" refers to the action of trading in response to breaking news. Consider the acquisition of Nord Anglia Education Inc., a Hong Kong-based operator of international schools, by the Canada Pension Plan Investment Board and Baring Private Equity Asia for US$4.3 billion on Tuesday, April 25, 2017. According to the company's website, the positive news of the acquisition had caused the price of

Nord Anglia Education Inc. (NORD) shares to jump by 17.38 percent by 10:00 a.m. on the same day.

A trader will profit handsomely if he or she takes a suitable position based on news and is able to capitalize on momentum early on. A trader, on the other hand, who takes the wrong position or continues to maintain the wrong position in the face of negative news, may incur huge losses. As a consequence, traders who base their judgments on black swan events stand to profit or lose a lot of money, depending on whether they choose the right position or not.

Consider the hypothetical circumstance below. Consider a poorly managed state-owned oil company that was on the verge of going bankrupt and was publicly traded. Assume the news was aired on the radio or television. When customers hear such news, their natural reaction is to sell their shares in the state-owned oil company, which is understandable. Consider the case of a shareholder in a state-owned oil company who learnt about the company's troubles the day before it was reported on the news. They would be able to sell off all of their shares and make a higher profit than if they had waited for the news. As a consequence, trading based on news would be more beneficial to the retail trader than trading without considering news.

It is vital to understand that insider trading occurs when stakeholders in a company trade based on information that has not yet been publicly released. Such behavior is considered unethical and is illegal in many countries throughout the globe.

Significant news has a propensity to increase the amount of trade in the affected shares, currency pairs, and financial assets. Because the forex market's volatility tends to grow when major news is released, many forex brokers attempt to widen the spread between the bid and ask price when this happens. The bid and ask prices are regarded equal if the gap between two currency pairs is made up of a bid price of US$1.258 and an ask price of US$1.260. The difference between US$1.258 and US$1.260 is 0.0002 (or 2 pip), or 1%.

Market orders may be filled at a price that is significantly different from the price that the retail trader intended to pay during times of news-related volatility. Consider the following illustration: A currency pair's ask price is US$1.260. If a trader feels that the bid price will rise to a level considerably higher than US$1.260 in the future, he or she might go long and buy the currency pair. Consider the case below: During a moment of particularly high volatility, a trader puts a long market order. It's possible that the order will be fulfilled at a bid price that's much greater than the current ask price of US$1.260. As a result, in order for the trader to benefit, the market would have to climb even higher in order to cover the bid-ask spread as well as the cost of charge.

On the downside, a similar problem might emerge, causing a profit slippage for ordinary traders. Consider still another scenario. Assume that a trader anticipating a market decline placed a short market order for the currency pair in this scenario. Assume the order was placed at a period of high market volatility. It's possible that the order may be filled at a considerably lower price than the trader expected, resulting in slippage.

It's worth remembering that financial markets don't always respond in the same manner once major market news is released. Large jumps and long candlesticks may define price movement in both directions (Lahaye et al. 2011). During instances of significant volatility in the news market, it's possible that delays in order processing may occur. Traders might lose money even though their orders are placed at the precise time. This is because delays in processing orders might result in losses for traders. Consider the case below: A retail trader placed a long order for a currency pair at US$1.260 with the goal of profitably shorting it at US$1.270. Assume there was a hitch in the order's completion, and when it was ultimately filled, the currency pair's price soared to US$1.501. Let's say there was another increase to US$1.265 after that. Because the long order was filled at a far higher price than the short order, the transaction was not profitable for the retail trader.

A retail trader should be aware of the volatility-related risks of news trading, which have previously been described. As a preventive step, retail traders may use limit orders with target profits to help minimize volatility risk during periods of substantial news-related volatility.

Heikin-Ashi.

Heikin-Ashi charts, rather than the more conventional candlestick charts, are preferred by some day traders for detecting patterns. Heikin-Ashi charts, in fact, may be used for a range of trading strategies, including crossovers, momentum, and reversals. The trader's tolerance for getting false signals determines whether or not Heikin-Ashi charts should be used. The great majority of firms who offer online trading interfaces for their consumers will display prices as Heikin-Ashi candlesticks.

Considering the trading technique.

It's critical for traders to evaluate their trading methods in order to determine if they're working and where they might improve. The trader needs keep track of the following facts in order to do such an evaluation:

• on a daily basis, the size of the average victory or loss profit or loss on average

• on a per-unit basis, the size of the average loss

• The winning-to-losing ratio is the average level of risk borne on each contract.

• the total number of round-trips completed in one day

Only by properly quantifying the gains, losses, and dangers connected with a trading strategy can it be evaluated successfully. Retail traders will be able to determine their daily profitability based on their average profit. When earnings are inadequate, or losses occur, trading tactics should be updated.

The average magnitude of the gain indicates the best time for the trader to keep the position open before closing it, and vice versa. The quantity of the gains may show whether or not the trader is closing winning positions too quickly, assuming that the amount of financial capital moved stays constant. Similarly, the average loss size may be used to identify whether a trader is holding losing positions for an inordinate length of time. Traders may change their strategy after receiving such information and opt to hold profitable positions for a longer period of time. They may also use a more stringent risk management strategy in order to limit their losses.

A trader may evaluate their trading success by reviewing their trades from the previous day/week and asking themselves the following questions:

•   Was there a strategy for creating and closing positions? Was it followed, if that's the case?

•   If so, whatever technical or fundamental analytical approaches were used to inform trading decisions?

•   Was there a target amount of wins or losses to achieve?

•   Was trading suspended or ended earlier than expected?

•   Were losing positions held for a longer amount of time than the plan called for?

•   Is it feasible that any of the trading choices were influenced by human emotion?

The answers to the simple questions above may provide useful insight into why a trader is losing money.

A trader's trading strategy may be scrutinized more thoroughly using more complex tools like the Sharpe Ratio and Monte Carlo simulation, both of which are accessible to him. While competent traders with a background in financial economics may utilize such complex tactics, they are beyond the scope of this book, which is intended at new and inexperienced traders.

Trading efficiently over time with a goal and winning strategy is very difficult for a trader to attain. The essential components of a trading strategy were examined in the first portion of this chapter. These include, among other things, entry and departure restrictions, risk management standards, and position size requirements.

Following that, this chapter looked at a number of simple trading strategies. Cross-overs, momentum, and reversal trading were shown to be the most successful trading strategies. Moving Average Envelopes, Bollinger Bands, and Heikin-Ashi charts, on the other hand, may be utilized to supplement the information offered by these indicators. While indicators may be useful in trading, it's important to realize that an indication isn't the same as a trading strategy.

Finally, this chapter addressed a basic framework for measuring the effectiveness of applied trading systems. Simple trading strategies are easy to create, implement, and assess. They are also rather affordable. Complex techniques, on the other hand, are more difficult to create, test, and optimize since they need more time and effort. The same concept holds true for assessment methods as for other sorts of evaluation. As previously said, this book focuses on simple methods since the target audience is the seasoned reader looking to expand their financial knowledge and awareness.

Chapter Six

Charting

A chart is a visual representation of an item's pricing over time. A price point, a pricing scale, and a time scale are all features of it.

For day traders, the price scale may be viewed on the right side of the chart. The scale goes from lowest to highest from top to bottom. Despite its fundamental basis, the price scale may have a complicated structure.

The distance between price points in a linear pricing system is the same. All price points will be the same if the difference between the first and second pricing points is 10. In a logarithmic pricing system, the distance between two price points equals the same percentage change. This means that a 25% price adjustment will have an equivalent impact on all price points.

The time scale is a date or time range presented at the bottom of the chart. If the day trader picks a shorter time, he may expect a more detailed chart with each data point reflecting the asset's closing price. Certain charts may display the open, high, low, and closing prices.

In a single trading session, an intraday chart illustrates price variations over a certain time period. A day trader would expect a five-minute time period or less. On a daily chart, a series of price movements may be viewed, with each trading session represented by a single point, which might be the open, high, low, or closing price.

Charts are available in a range of sizes and shapes:

Open-High-Low-Close (OHLC).

These charts, which are also known as bar charts, depict the connection between the highest and lowest prices during a trading session. A tick on the left side usually represents the open price, while a tick on the right side usually represents the closing price.

Diagram with Figures and Points

Instead of utilizing time to produce the chart, numerical filters are used to relate to times.

Overlays.

These may be seen on most major price charts and come in a number of formats:

• Resistance is a price level that works as a maximum level above the typical price.

• The polar opposite of resistance is support, which appears as the lowest price value.

• A trend line connects two peaks or troughs on a graph.

• A channel is defined as two trend lines that are parallel to each other.

• A moving average is a dynamic trend line that looks at the average price of the market.

• Bollinger bands are charts that show how volatile the market is.

- A pivot point is the average of the high, low, and closing price averages for a given stock or currency.

Indicators depending on the price.

These look at how the market prices things. Here are a few examples:

- Market breadth is measured by the advance decline line.

- The average directional index (ADI) is a market trend strength indicator.

- The commodity channel index is a tool for detecting market cyclical trends.

- The relative strength index (RSI) is a chart that shows how strong a price is.

- The moving average convergence indicator shows when two trend lines converge or diverge (MACD).

- The stochastic oscillator (SOC) shows the trading range's most recent closing position.

- A momentum chart depicts how rapidly the price changes.

Heiken-Ashi.

In Heiken-Ashi outlines, candles are utilized as the charting medium, but the cost is calculated differently. Instead of using candles decoded from core open-high-low-close criteria, costs are smoothed to make it more likely to show inclining value action, as shown by this equation.

Close = (Open + High + Low + Close)/4 Lowest of the Lows, Open, or Close = (Open of previous bar + Close of previous bar)/2

Consistent terminology.

The average real range is the range over a certain period of time, generally one day at a time.

Breakout — When a security's value regularly bursts through a zone of support or resistance owing to an expected flood of buying or selling volume.

Cycle - A set of time periods throughout which value activities must follow a certain pattern.

When the value of a property falls in a down market, purchasers may take a minor discount or sell exaggeratedly, resulting in a rise in cost. The momentary purchasing spell is nicknamed a dead feline skip when traders force the market farther down.

The Dow Theory is used to support the average premise. According to proponents of the hypothesis, if one of them goes off, the other will most likely follow. Many traders monitor the transportation industry because it may provide information about the economy's health. The existence of a big number of goods shipments and exchanges implies a healthy economy.

Doji - A flame type with a little variation between the open and closing price, reflecting market apprehension.

Markets go through cycles of good faith and skepticism, according to Elliott wave theory, which may be foreseen and utilized to prepare for trading opportunities.

Fibonacci proportions are a set of numbers that may be used to calculate support and opposition.

Sounds - Harmonic trading is founded on the idea that value designs repeat themselves, and that defining market moments may be detected using Fibonacci sequences.

Candlestick charts

Candlestick charts are easy to understand and use, and they provide the most information to traders by showing where a price moves over time. They also allow him or her to incorporate information regarding certain time periods. He or she can identify the highest and lowest price points, as well as the most recent closing price, in this case.

Candlesticks aid traders in obtaining accurate visual readings of the market by providing just the most important information, such as the Heikin-Ashi chart, which shows trends and reversals. Different candlestick charts illustrate various market aspects, such as time, volume, and price movements.

To help day traders identify resistance and support levels, certain candlestick charts focus only on price fluctuations. The highest trading highs are represented by the resistance levels, while the lowest trading lows are represented by the support levels. Renko is a kind of candlestick chart in which trading patterns are represented by colored bricks.

The visible blocks are black when there is a downward trend, and they are white when there is an upward trend. The bricks also move in reaction to price changes, with a new white or black block emerging in the next column if the price goes chevalier.

Other candlestick charts may help a day trader detect reversal points, swing highs and lows, and swing highs and lows. These charts assist him in identifying areas and circumstances where market bias exists, enabling him to take appropriate measures that result in gains. A Kagi chart, for example, uses price direction changes to signal reversals.

The intraday trader selects a specified reversal amount when the price reaches that preset percentage, and the price direction switches to the opposite side. The high and low line signals also illustrate swings, with the lines becoming thinner as the market falls below the previous swing. When the stock climbs over the prior swing, on the other hand, the line thickens.

Bar charts.

For day traders, bar charts combine color, horizontal, and vertical lines to illustrate a range or price over time, making them simpler to read and analyze. The horizontal lines indicate the closing and opening prices, while the vertical lines indicate the price range for a certain time period. Traders may combine them with candlestick charts to show market trading activity.

The trading range is represented by the difference between the low and high of a bar using candlesticks. The top of the candle or wick represents the high state, while the bottom of the candle or wick represents the low condition. Furthermore, the chart uses different colors on the candlestick to depict the opening and closing prices throughout time. The closing price at the low end and the opening price at the high end may be represented by a red candle. In contrast to a red candle, a green candle reflects its prices in the other way.

Line graphs.

By presenting a track of the market's closing prices, line charts give an intraday trader with a price history. Lines are formed when a trader joins multiple closing costs throughout a certain time period. To acquire vital data for a successful Day Trading session, he or she uses line charts, as well as other forms of trading charts.

Graphs with various time periods.

The time periods on a day trader's trading charts are all set according to his or her aims or trading tactics. The trader has access to intraday charts, which are separated into 2-minute, 5-minute, 15-minute, and hourly charts. Each time interval reflects an interest transaction's price fluctuations, and he or she may use the data to make proper trading decisions and moves.

Free charts are available.

Intraday traders may get free charts on the internet, which feature not only technical analysis tools but also assistance, demonstrations, and chart interpretation instructions. Free charts include features such as delayed futures data, real-time data, and the option to choose time frames and indicators. A trader may use these charts to trade in a range of markets, including forex, futures, stock exchanges, and stocks. Two examples of free charts that an intraday trader may acquire and utilize without spending any money are the Technician and Free Stock Charts.

Chapter Seven

Diversification of the Portfolio

Investors purchase and keep equities for days, weeks, months, and even years, while day traders undertake transactions over the length of a single trading day. Other types of business exist between these two extremes. Swing and position trading are two types of trading that fall within this category. I highly urge readers to diversify their trading accounts and incorporate a mid or long-term strategy in addition to day trading options techniques to decrease overall portfolio volatility. Because of the significant inherent leverage of options and day trading tactics in general, you will examine portfolio diversification fundamentals here. If you are a total beginner, depending only on day trading tactics will result in significant losses over time. Swing trading is when a trader buys and maintains a commodity or equity position for a few days before selling it. Position trading is when a trader acquires a position in a commodity or stock for a period of weeks or months. While all of these activities are risky, day trading is the most dangerous.

A trader with the required abilities and access to all resources will almost certainly succeed, but the learning curve will be steep. Professional day traders, whether they operate for themselves or for major businesses, work full time. They typically create a timetable that they strictly follow. Being a part-time day trader, hobby trader, or gambler is never a smart idea. You must trade full-time and be as disciplined as possible to succeed.

Diversification is a broad phrase that refers to a variety of ideas.

Diversification is considered a good risk management strategy. Both traders and investors utilize it extensively. This strategy is based on the idea that investing in a single asset is particularly hazardous since the whole transaction might go bankrupt or result in huge losses.

An optimal asset portfolio is predicted to return much more than a non-diversified portfolio. Even when comparing returns on lower-risk products like bonds, this is true. Diversification is suggested not only to boost profits but also to protect against losses in general.

Fundamentals of Diversification

Traders and investors buy and sell stocks on stock exchanges. One of the risks of investing in the stock market is that most traders will only hold one or two equities at a time. This is dangerous because if a transaction fails, the trader might lose everything. Diversification, on the other hand, distributes risk so that the trader may benefit regardless of what happens to certain assets.

Diversification is predicated on the difficulty provided by unpredictable threats. These risks are decreased when some firms or investments outperform others. As a consequence, a trader should only deal with non-correlated assets in order to maintain a properly balanced portfolio. This implies that the assets operate in a manner that is opposing or distinct from market forces.

Between 25 and 30 equities should make up the perfect portfolio. This is a fantastic method for avoiding risk and guaranteeing that profits are the sole anticipated consequence.

Finally, diversification is a common trading and investing approach. It invests in a diverse range of assets in order to maximize returns while minimizing inherent and possible risks.

Investing or trading in a range of assets rather than a single kind is preferred. Currency, options, shares, bonds, and other assets, for example, should all be included in a well-diversified portfolio. This strategy will boost earning potential while reducing risk and exposure. Even more diversity is provided by assets acquired in various regions of the globe.

The most successful method is diversification.

Asset allocation emphasizes diversification. It is a means of allocating funds or assets to various investments in the most efficient manner possible. An investor who diversifies his or her portfolio must be ready to accept some risk. However, the investor should design an exit plan so that they may return their investment by selling the asset. This is crucial when a particular asset class does not deliver appropriate returns when compared to others.

An investor's investment will be appropriately protected if they can build a well-diversified portfolio. Future growth is also possible with a well-diversified portfolio. It's critical to maintain a well-balanced portfolio since various assets respond differently to market downturns. It helps investors manage portfolio volatility and leverage risk.

Diversification is a big issue among investors.

Various investors have different notions about what circumstances are best for investment. Regardless of market circumstances, many investors feel that a well-diversified portfolio will almost certainly earn a double-digit return. They also agree that in the worst-case situation, the value of the different assets would just decrease. Even with all of this knowledge, only a tiny percentage of investors are able to diversify their portfolios.

Why can't investors just diversify their investments as they see fit? The replies are intriguing and varied. When diversifying their portfolios, investors face a number of obstacles, including weighting mismatch, hidden connection, underlying devaluation, and misleading outcomes. While these problems seem to be complicated, they are simple to resolve. Similarly, the solution is straightforward. By overcoming these obstacles, an investor will be able to reap the advantages of a well-diversified platform.

The Allocation of Asset Classes Process

Assets may be allocated to investments in a number of ways. Most investors, even professional investors, portfolio managers, and seasoned traders, seldom outperform their chosen asset class benchmarks, according to research. It's also worth noting that the performance of an underlying asset class and the returns of an investor are tightly connected. Professional investors do almost as well as an index within the same asset class.

A diversified portfolio's investment returns should, on average, closely match those of the relevant asset class. As a consequence, asset class selection is considered a critical component of every investment. It is, in fact, the single most important factor in determining an asset class's success. Other variables such as asset selection and market timing only account for around 6% of the variation in investing results.

Diversification of assets across several asset classes.

Diversification simply means investing in a variety of securities from a variety of industries, including health care, financial services, and energy, as well as medium, small, and large-cap companies. This is a typical investor's viewpoint. However, a deeper examination of this strategy indicates that investors are just diversifying their stock market investments. When the markets rise and fall, certain asset kinds may readily fall and rise.

Due to the hidden links that exist between different asset classes, a well-diversified portfolio needs knowledge and alertness on the part of the investor or even the portfolio manager. This connection is prone to vary throughout time for a number of reasons. The presence of worldwide markets is one of the causes. Many investors buy foreign equities to diversify their portfolios.

On the other hand, there is a clear link between the various global financial markets. This link may be seen in developing markets all across the globe, not only in Europe. The link between stocks and fixed income markets, two of the most important components of diversification, is substantial.

This correlation is troublesome since it is almost certainly the effect of structured finance and investment banking interacting. The great expansion and popularity of hedge funds is another element that adds to this relationship. Consider the loss of a big worldwide corporation in a certain asset class, such as a hedge fund.

If this occurs, the company may be required to liquidate assets across many asset types. This will have a multiplier effect since many other assets will be affected, and other investors will lose money despite having well-diversified portfolios. A huge percentage of investors are likely to be ignorant of this issue. They're also unlikely to know how to fix or avoid it.

The practice of realigning asset classes is referred to as "asset class realignment."

Concentrating on class realignment is one of the most successful ways to tackle the correlation issue. In general, asset allocation should not be seen as a one-dimensional process. Asset class imbalance arises when the securities markets mature and various asset classes perform differently.

Over time, investors should review their investments and diversify out of failing assets, reinvesting in asset classes that are doing well and lucrative. Nonetheless, since other conventional risks remain, it's important to keep an eye on things to make sure no one asset type is over-represented. A protracted bull market may lead to an overvaluation of one or more asset classes, indicating that a correction is due. A range of strategies are available to an investor, which are covered further down.

Relative Value and Diversification

Even experienced investors have learned that asset returns may be deceiving at times. As a consequence, asset returns should be considered in the context of the performance of the corresponding asset class. When evaluating the statistics, keep in mind the underlying currency as well as the risks that this asset class confronts.

When diversifying your investments, think about dividing them into asset groups with various risk profiles. These should be kept in many currencies. When it comes to government bonds and technological businesses, don't anticipate the same outcomes. However, you must try to understand how each one fits into your overall investment strategy.

You will be able to earn more from a little gain from an asset inside a market where the currency is growing in value if you use this method. This is in contrast to a large profit on an asset in a market where the currency is dropping. As a consequence, large profits might be converted into losses when transferred to a stronger currency. This is why thorough study and appraisal of different asset types is critical.

Currency considerations are essential.

When determining which asset classes to diversify into, currency considerations are critical. Take, for example, the Swiss franc. It has been one of the most stable currencies in the world since the 1940s. As a consequence, this money may be used to track the performance of other currencies in a safe and reliable manner.

On the other hand, private investors may commit an excessive amount of time on stock selection and trading. These projects are time intensive and frightening. As a consequence, it is preferable to take a different strategy in such cases and concentrate more on the asset class. This strategy has the potential to be far more lucrative. Successful investing requires proper asset allocation. It helps investors to reduce portfolio volatility while lowering investment risks. This is because various asset classes respond differently to different market circumstances.

It is feasible to develop a stable and lucrative portfolio that beats the index of assets by building a well-thought-out and adequately diversified portfolio. Leverage may also be used by investors to mitigate any risks that may arise as a consequence of shifting market circumstances.

To give you an example.

An investor makes a $100,000 investment. The best way to invest money is in a broad portfolio, but balancing the portfolio effectively and enough is difficult. Before weighing prospective benefits against potential hazards, the first step is to examine market circumstances. As a consequence, the investor may put his money into very secure assets that are expected to pay off in the long run.

A well-diversified portfolio of 10 to 12 shares might be included in such an investment. Typically, they are equities from a variety of firms, industry, and nations. Diversification like this helps to hedge against possible risks while still keeping a well-balanced portfolio.

Investing with discipline is essential.

Everyone feels that variety is the most successful strategy. However, when it comes to investing and diversifying your portfolio, you must apply investor discipline. Investing is a fine art. Put part of your money into stocks, but not all of it. Instead, imagine yourself as a mutual fund manager putting together an investment portfolio. You may also invest in real estate investment trusts (REITs) and exchange-traded funds (ETFs) (exchange-traded funds). It's also a good idea to invest worldwide rather than locally. In this approach, you diversify your risk and boost your chances of profit.

Both bonds and index funds are wonderful investments.

A trader may invest in fixed-income or index funds in addition to stocks from various businesses. You should invest in securities that closely resemble a major index since you will be able to watch your investments and track their progress. These funds are inexpensive and make it simple to keep track of your money.

Portfolio construction is a never-ending process.

Always try to increase the value of your belongings. If you are given money, you should consider putting part of it into your investing portfolio. Maintain a consistent investment schedule for your portfolio. You might, for example, donate $500 each month to help this portfolio develop faster.

Learn when the best moments to depart are.

The buy-and-hold strategy has become second nature to us. This is particularly true when our investments are set up to run on autopilot.

Even if you are a cautious investor, you must keep an eye out for occurrences and unusual conditions. Maintain constant awareness of current events and be prepared to respond in any circumstance. When the time comes, you'll be ready to reduce your losses and exit your trades if you do it this manner.

Keep an eye out for commission employment possibilities.

You should be informed of the commissions, fees, and charges that must be paid as a trader. These expenses might potentially add up to a substantial amount. As a consequence, keep an eye on the pricing to ensure that they remain within reason. Investing should be educational, amusing, rewarding, and instructive in general.

To be successful in the long term and perhaps beat some of the main indexes, you must be a disciplined trader. You should diversify your portfolio, continue to enhance it, and learn to read indications and understand when to quit a transaction in addition to the buy-and-hold method. Your trading operations will be fairly beneficial in the long term if you trade in this method.

Contextual Diversification

In a single statement, diversification may be defined. You should never put all of your eggs in one basket. This is as straightforward as it gets. However, the text does not specify how diversity should be attained.

Portfolio diversification is a straightforward concept. A trader should diversify among a wide variety of securities, preferably across many asset classes. A portfolio made up entirely of stocks from one firm would be inappropriate. If anything bad happens to that firm, the investor or trader stands to lose a lot of money, which might put a trader's investing or trading goals on hold.

When a single investment is spread among two or more companies and asset classes, the risk associated with it is greatly decreased. Diversifying your portfolio with bonds, futures, and currencies is a smart idea in addition to investing in a range of companies.

Traders must devise a strategy for allocating their assets. Stock and bond investment should be the major emphasis of such a strategy. Asset allocation and diversification are intertwined because, when done correctly, asset allocation produces a continuously varied portfolio.

There are many changes that may be made to assist safeguard and diversify a portfolio. This is a mutual fund that invests in a diverse variety of assets. Diversifying into a mutual fund, which is often a diversified investment, may assist to further diversify a portfolio.

It's a good idea to learn how to calculate a decent risk-to-reward ratio. This ratio may assist you in determining the best approach to diversify your assets. A risk-reward ratio permits those who are prepared to take a little amount of risk to obtain a certain rate of return. As a consequence, persons who are prepared to take on greater risk have a better chance of success than those who are not.

Some individuals pick lower risk levels due to a lack of cash or a desire to have the fewest potential consequences. These investors merely replicate the performance of a single, well-balanced fund. Others just make a donation to the fund. Others, on the other hand, may find this strategy too simple and prefer a more varied approach.

Finally, diversity is critical for long-term financial success. Not only is it more lucrative, but it also includes risk management in the portfolio management process. Finding a good balance in the assets you choose to diversify your portfolio is an excellent way to go about it.

Day Trading Risks Can Be Minimized

Risk management is an important part of any transaction, despite the fact that it is often disregarded. On that day, traders must learn about risk management if they want to trade effectively and profitably in the long term. The good news is that there are a few basic procedures that may be performed to guarantee transaction security and risk management.

Risk management is one of the most crucial components of every serious day trader's life. The rationale for this is that although 90% of a trader's transactions are successful, the remaining 10% might result in a net loss if risk management is not properly controlled. As a consequence, it's vital to properly plan all transactions and take precautions to safeguard all trades against losses.

Trades need considerable planning.

It is common knowledge that a well-planned strategy, rather than a victorious combat, will win the war. The first stage for a good day trader is to plan and build a lucrative strategy. "Plan the trade and trade the plan," said a lot of traders. This is analogous to war preparation in that those that plan ahead of time are more likely to win.

Conclusion

It is possible to combine it with your current job or pursue it as a full-time profession. If you want to be a day trader, the concept is that you can work whenever and wherever you choose. You may schedule your day as you choose, and you can work from home or while traveling.

It's a little business that doesn't need a lot of funding to get started. The initial investments are a computer, a few monitors, a fast and steady internet connection, and trading software. They're also cost-effective.

You have no duties to anybody as a full-time trader. As an independent contractor, you are responsible to no one but yourself. You don't have a dictatorial boss who checks to see whether you're working out the window of his office. When you're unwell, you may choose to spend the whole day in bed.

The best thing about day trading is that you may develop a style that suits your personality, is laid-back, and suits your temperament. Take a day off when the market gets too volatile to handle and complete any lingering tasks, such as house maintenance, cooking, or visiting a family member or friend. You may spend the money you saved by avoiding a risky market on your children, errands, or shopping.

The greatest aspect of choosing day trading as a strategy to generate money is that it does not need a degree or any special expertise. You'll need to drink up a lot of knowledge before declaring yourself ready for active trading, but no certification is required. There are various free online sites that might help you broaden your financial knowledge base.

You may register for them. Combining online research with reading a good book is the best method.

Another benefit of day trading is that you may work from home. You work from the comfort of your own home while sipping your coffee. To carry out your transactions, you don't need permission from anybody higher up. Profits are your responsibility, as is the method in which the transaction is carried out.

The ability to sleep comfortably is one of the most enticing advantages of being a day trader. All of your transactions are closed at the end of the day. There is no risk of losing money overnight. There's no way your stock value will collapse to nothing while you're buried in the valley of dreams. Day trading gives you more earnings certainty and control over your trading company. You can sleep comfortably at night if everything went well throughout the day and you earned enough money.

Made in the USA
Middletown, DE
13 September 2024

60916667R00062